# The Clinical Teaching Model

*Clinical Insights and
Strategies for the
Learning-Disabled Child*

# The Clinical Teaching Model

*Clinical Insights and Strategies for the Learning-Disabled Child*

by
## Selma G. Sapir, Ed.D.
*Senior Faculty Member and Psychologist,
Graduate Programs in Learning Disability;
Director, Learning Lab,
Bank Street College of Education,
New York*

 BRUNNER/MAZEL, *Publishers* • New York

**Library of Congress Cataloging in Publication Data**

Sapir, Selma G.
    Clinical insights and strategies for the
learning-disabled child.

    Bibliography: p.
    Includes index.
    1. Learning disabilities. 2. Handicapped
children—Psychology. 3. Tutors and tutoring.
4. Child psychotherapy. 5. Psychotherapist and
patient. I. Title. [DNLM: 1. Teaching—methods.
2. Education, Special. 3. Learning Disorders.
4. Psychology, Educational. LC 4704 S241c]
LC4704.S257    1985        371.9             84-21365

ISBN 0-87630-383-1

Copyright © 1985 by Selma G. Sapir

*Published by*

**BRUNNER/MAZEL, Inc.**
19 Union Square West
New York, N.Y. 10003

MANUFACTURED IN THE UNITED STATES OF AMERICA

To Dr. Lawrence Cremin, former President of Teachers College, Columbia University, for the many ways in which he offered his assistance

# Contents

# Introduction

In the practice of psychotherapy some links have been drawn between theory and practice, but rarely have educational treatment models been tied to the underlying principles of philosophies or theories. The purpose of this book is to explore the many philosophies and theories in psychology in order to determine whether the contributions set forth in the literature have relevance for the formulation of a new model for the treatment of learning-disabled children.

Behaviorism, psychoanalysis, self-actualization, and the developmental-interaction philosophies are presented, and their significance to the needs of learning-disabled children is evaluated. The developmental theories of Gesell, Erikson, Hebb, Piaget, Vygotsky, Luria, and Werner are introduced as a guide to help formulate an integrative position and to understand "deviation from the norm" as commonly used in the learning disability literature. An attempt is made to develop ways to implement theoretical contributions in a new treatment model: the Clinical Teaching Model.

To generate this new model, certain principles may be relevant to its development:

1) Growth in any one area chains with growth in all areas (social, emotional and cognitive).
2) As children mature, the way they respond to tasks shifts. Maturation implies a continuous process of change.
3) Assessment may be seen as an uninterrupted flow of information derived from observations of children as they mature and develop.
4) To understand deviation from the norm, one must be cognizant of normal developmental theories.
5) The selection and pairing of children and tutors by identifying certain characteristics, such as temperament, personality, and cognitive style, may enable the adult to become a model for the child to emulate.
6) The dyadic relationship of tutor and child may play an important therapeutic role, thus enhancing learning and growth.

The need for a new model is real because present models have not brought positive results while, at the same time, the number of children with learning disability continues to mount. This demands an examination of what already exists in treatment methodology so that successful components of existing models can be combined to develop a new approach.

The large number of learning-disabled children makes it essential to study the many causes of these problems and to identify methods of assessing children that will protect them from the stigma of labeling. Many of these children, with proper training, may function well in later life regardless of the cause of their early academic problems.

As one examines what is being offered as treatment models, it is noted that most emphasize cognitive training, disregarding other aspects of the child's life. Some offer psychotherapeutic training, again in isolation from other important factors. There have been very few attempts in work with learning-disabled children to integrate the social, cognitive, and affective needs of these youngsters.

The Clinical Teaching Model approaches treatment from a developmental-interaction perspective (Shapiro & Biber, 1973), which suggests that growth in any one area chains with growth in all areas (social, emotional, and cognitive). It assumes that what is communicated between two people (tutor and child) may have a profound and everlasting effect on the way the child and/or adult approach many aspects of their life, including academic learning. Because of this, the model stresses the importance of considering certain fundamental characteristics, such as temperament, personality, and cognitive style, when selecting and pairing children and tutors.

With the Clinical Teaching Model, assessment is seen as a continuous process involving more than diagnostic tests. Assessment, treatment strategies, and evaluation are interwoven, allowing for constant refinement of the treatment process. As the child grows, so must the treatment strategies change.

This book emphasizes the role of the tutor-child dyad, but in no way does it minimize the need for "diagnostic counseling" for the parents, teachers, and all others who interact with the child. Sapir and Wilson (1978) emphasize the counseling role of professionals and state that every contact should be perceived as an opportunity to support and guide the family and teachers who are in contact with the child daily.

Many controversial issues in the field of learning disabilities will be presented, as well as some definitions of terms. The Clinical Teaching Model is derived from components of several theories. It draws heavily from basic child development theories and attempts to integrate these theories with remedial cognitive and psychotherapeutic practices. Whereas other models have followed one or more of these practices, the Clinical Teaching Model is interactive, integrated, and developmental in its perspective. It emphasizes the need for a dynamic relationship between tutor and child, which is viewed as a prerequisite for enhanced growth in each member of the dyad. This relationship is embedded in treatment strategies that focus on cognitive and academic issues, even while they attend to the child's social and emotional needs.

As stated earlier, The Clinical Teaching Model draws from the developmental theories of Gesell, Anna Freud, Erikson, Hebb, Piaget, Vygotsky, Luria, and Werner. One of the basic tenets of this Model is that one must understand normal development before one can understand deviation from the norm. Each of the theorists presented considers a different aspect of the child—behavior, emotion, physiology, language, neurology, and biology—but all aspects are important in the child's development.

Maturation implies change, and even when there is delayed development the organism changes with age. It is because of this that the Clinical Teaching Model presumes that diagnosis is an ongoing process. As children mature, the way they function shifts (Piaget, 1955). The model also assumes that the best diagnosticians are those professionals who work with children on a regular basis so that they can observe the performance of the child and adjust treatment accordingly. Assessment is also seen in an interactive, developmental mode so that temperament, physical characteristics, affect, social factors, language, perception, and cognition are as important as the academic performance.

Another principle of the Clinical Teaching Model is the importance of the selection and pairing of tutor and child. It suggests that criteria for such a selection and pairing be determined by the need of the child to have an adult who can become a model for the child's efforts. The tutor in some ways compensates for the difficulties the child experiences, and sets an example of a better way to perform. The tutor does not impose this on the child but rather exemplifies another way to behave. For example, if the child is impulsive and poorly organized, a tutor who is reflective and well organized would be selected. If, on the other hand, the child is obsessive and compulsive, a tutor who is very adaptable and flexible would be suggested.

This book focuses on the importance of the dynamic relationship: the interactive communication between the adult tutor and child. Because it stresses the reciprocal influence each member of the dyad has on the other, a pilot study is presented in an attempt to show the relationship between the interactive communication system of the tutor-child dyad and its growth. Through the study of tutor-child relationships taken from "cinéma vérité" videotapes made prior to the study, it may be possible to see the effect of the interactions between tutors and children on later academic achievement. If positive interactions enhance academic achievement and developmental growth, then it follows that tutor training in positive verbal and nonverbal communications must become an inherent part of the training model.

The last three chapters of this book comprise three case examples to exemplify the Clinical Teaching Model. It is hoped that application of this model will enable more children to reach their potential and become successful members of the adult community.

It should be noted that the child is referred to as "he" in the text, in order to free the writing from awkwardness.

## ACKNOWLEDGMENTS

The author wishes to express her gratitude to all the graduate students who participated in the Learning Lab and to the many administrators at Bank Street College who made it possible.

Special thanks go to Kay Greenspan, Leila Javitch, and Ann Welborn (Supervisors), all of whom organized and presented the case studies reproduced in this book.

# The Clinical
# Teaching Model

*Clinical Insights and*
*Strategies for the*
*Learning-Disabled Child*

# CHAPTER I

# Controversial Issues and Definitions in Learning Disability

Many controversial issues in the education of handicapped children remain unresolved. Changes in philosophy, programming, and educational methodology have been so rapid as to cause confusion and controversy in the field. How one views these crucial issues will determine how the learning-disabled child is defined, how his deficits are conceptualized, and on what basis the remediation has been predicated.

The concept of "brain damage" first began to make an impact on the educational scene with the work of Alfred Strauss and Laura Lehtinen (1947), Heinz Werner (1948), and Newell Kephart (1968). The "brain-damaged" era began slowly with the publishing of Strauss and Lehtinen's book in 1947 but did not emerge fully until the early 1960s. In the late 1950s and early 1960s, many research physicians became aware of a population without "frank brain damage" but with many of the same symptoms.

In 1962, I began my research in a normal public school setting (Sapir, 1971). As a psychologist, I had become aware of increasing numbers of children with uneven and deviant cognitive, social, and emotional growth patterns. Early identification of these children with the Sapir Developmental Scale (Sapir & Wilson, 1967) highlighted widely divergent patterns of deficits in youngsters of normal to superior intelligence with a gross imbalance in developmental milestones. Boys seemed to have many more difficulties than girls.

As the body of research developed, many disciplines began to coalesce in the emergence of a new educational concept: learning disabilities. At the same time, parents began to exert their efforts to develop educational programs suitable for children having severe problems in school. Children were described along a continuum from seemingly normal with reading problems to profoundly disabled with many dysfunctions. Early attempts to integrate the disciplines of education, medicine, and behavioral science were unsuccessful because of the difficulties of definition.

The necessity of defining a vastly diverse population has led to some arbitrary differentiations of the children now described as having "learning disability," "minimal brain dysfunction," "minimal cerebral dysfunction," "dyslexia," "strephosymbolia," and about 50 other designations. In no other area of special education have so much effort and controversy gone into refinement of a definition. In 1966, a task force on terminology and identification of the child with "minimal brain dysfunction" was co-sponsored by the National Institute of Neurological Diseases and Blindness of the National Institute of Health. They defined it as follows:

> The term "minimal brain dysfunction syndrome" refers to the children of near average, average or above average general intelligence with certain learning or behavioral disabilities ranging from mild to severe which are associated with deviations of function of the central nervous system. These deviations may manifest themselves by various combinations of impairment in perception, conceptualization, language, memory and control of attention, impulse or motor function. Similar symptoms may or may not complicate the problems of children with cerebral palsy, epilepsy, mental retardation, blindness or deafness. (p. 8)

## DEFINITION OF LEARNING DISABILITY

The term "learning disability" means many different things depending on how and where it is used. Diagnosis and treatment, therefore, represent a vast array of etiologies and methodologies. To some it signifies all children who have achieved well below their developmental norm (some say one standard deviation, others two grades below expectation). To others it means those children who present some neurophysiological deviation from the norm. To still others it means a clustering of symptomatology conceived to be indicative of minimal brain dysfunction—e.g., soft signs such as hyperactivity, poor attention and concentration, small muscle motor dysfunction, and visual or auditory perceptual problems.

Because of the difficulty among professionals in reaching agreement as to the meaning of certain key words, the United States Office of Education and the World Federation of Neurology have provided a standard definition of learning disabilities as follows:

> Children with special learning disabilities exhibit a disorder in one or more of the basic psychological processes involved in understanding or in using spoken or written language. These may be manifested in disorders of listening, thinking, talking, reading, writing, spelling, or arithmetic.
>
> They include such conditions which have been referred to as perceptual handicaps, brain injuries, minimal brain dysfunction, dyslexia, developmental aphasias, etc.
>
> They do not include learning problems due primarily to visual, hearing or motor handicaps, to mental retardation, emotional disturbance, or to environmental disadvantage. (quoted in Sapir & Nitzburg, 1973, p. 157)

The problems of terminology are complicated by the need to satisfy many diverse demands of clinicians who diagnose, prescribe, or treat; researchers concerned with validity and reliability; educators who are held accountable; and parents and others personally involved with the child. A further complication lies in the fact that learning-disabled children can manifest varying degrees of severity from mild to profound and can show involvement in one or more specific areas, such as sensory motor perception and language development. These children reveal varying behavior patterns, from hyperactive to hypoactive, excellent motivation to little motivation, and perseverance to short attention span and high distractibility. Adding to the problem are the many terms used in the literature as described earlier.

How the term is defined and which children are being discussed, determine treatment methodology. Treatment procedures may be based on behavioral, psychoanalytic, self-actualizing, or developmental-interaction theories. The methodology chosen reflects the particular philosophical base from which one operates. A search of the literature reveals that research has seldom compared the different methodologies. An attempt will be made in the next chapter to highlight contrasting philosophies, instructional theories, and treatment models, including relevant research.

# CHAPTER 2

# Contrasting Philosophies, Instructional Theories, and Treatment Models

The models adopted for working with learning-disabled children reflect the bias of the developers in regard to principles underlying therapeutic change. In this chapter, the philosophical principles of behaviorism, psychoanalysis, self-actualization and developmental-interaction will be presented and evaluated for their relevance to the treatment of the learning-disabled child. Each has something to offer: behaviorism—the need for reinforcement; psychoanalysis—the child's defense system; self-actualization—the child's striving for competence and mastery; and developmental-interaction—the chaining of cognitive, emotional, and social growth patterns.

The ecological and decision-making models will also be discussed. They emphasize the importance of understanding the child in his or her environment (home, community, and school) and the need for the teacher or tutor to make decisions based on knowledge of the child's cognitive, emotional, and social stage of development. All these ideas have been incorporated into the Clinical Teaching Model.

## BEHAVIOR THERAPY

Behavior therapy is a term originally coined by Eysenck (1959) to denote a system of psychotherapy originated by Wolpe (1958). Its theoretical framework is based in learning theory which grew out of vigorously controlled laboratory experiments performed chiefly with animals. Behavior therapists have been largely interested in determining the functional relationships between experimental events. Overt behavior of a maladaptive type is seen as acquired or learned, and therefore, can be removed or unlearned in the same ways as it was originally acquired. Many of the current treatment models for exceptional children apply some of the principles of behaviorism.

Much of the theoretical base to behavior therapy stems from Skinner's (1938) work in "operant conditioning." Fundamental to the concept of operant conditioning is the idea, first, of choice and, second, of affecting or operating on the environment. The organism chooses one response over another because of the reinforcement which followed the act on previous occasions. Acts which are rewarded are learned, while acts which are punished or ignored are extinguished. In operant learning the stimulus represents a sign or use indicating the possibilities of reinforcement (reward or punishment) which the organism may elect to heed or not. Stimulus generalization occurs, and there is a range of environmental events likely to produce a learned response. The more similar the stimulus to the reinforced one, the more likely it is to be learned.

Werry and Wollersheim (1967) delineate seven phases of treatment as follows:

1) problem definition—selecting symptoms most distressing
2) problem analysis—determining the stimuli that elicit the symptoms
3) mapping out a plan of therapy by the behavior therapist
4) motivating the patient for therapy
5) behavior shaping—moving the child's behavior closer to de-

sired behavior in gradual steps whereby the therapist controls the stimuli and response

6) generalizing behavior—carrying the adaptive behaviors into natural settings such as home and school
7) stabilizing behavior—reinforcement to come from significant persons in child's environment

Techniques used by behavior therapists include manipulation of stimulus, response, and reinforcers, in addition to the manipulation of intra-organismic drive states. This latter involves manipulating the level and type of emotional state so that adaptive behaviors will appear.

## Disorders for Which Behavior Therapy Has Been Used

It is claimed that behavior therapy has been used successfully in eliminating undesirable behaviors in children with conduct disorders, impulsivity, emotional lability, attention problems, and poor academic performance. Among certain learning-disabled groups, a major problem seems to be a rebellious attitude toward the rules of society, resulting in poor conduct and possibly juvenile delinquency (Routh & Mesibov, 1980). Given the fact that these children are at risk for juvenile and adult antisocial behavior, behavior modification techniques have been suggested as a treatment model, with an emphasis on sensitizing the learning-disabled children to moral and ethical values as well as helping them with self-control and academic skills.

## Research with Behavior Therapy and Academic Performance

Quay, Werry, McQueen, and Sprague (1966) significantly improved classroom attention in conduct problem children by immediately reinforcing the desired behavior with light flashes followed by candy. Barrish, Saunder, and Wolf (1969), working with a single class of 24 fourth-grade students, demonstrated the effectiveness of what they called "the good behavior game." Out-of-seat behaviors and talking without permission during math and reading periods were the symptoms. The class was divided into two teams. Each instance of children out of their seats caused the team to have a mark against them which resulted in loss of privileges. Both teams could win if there were few enough marks against them. The procedure markedly reduced the negative target behaviors.

Meichenbaum and Goodman (1971), dealing with disruptive behavior in the classroom, taught a group of kindergarten and first-grade children several self-instructional techniques including verbal responses to disruptive situations. Their data suggest that this might be a relevant strategy to use with young children.

Allen, Henke, Harris, Baer, and Reynolds (1967) focused on increasing children's ability to attend and lessen impulsiveness. They worked successfully with a four-and-a-half-year-old boy with an excessively short attention span. After baseline observations were made, the child's nursery school teachers began to give attention and approval every time the child remained with an activity for one continuous minute or more. Within a week, according to Allen et al., the number of activity changes the child made went down markedly. Palkes, Stewart, and Kahana (1968) used visual reminder cards to teach hyperactive boys to "stop, look, and listen." The children gave themselves verbal commands out loud before each response on three different training tasks. The procedure significantly improved the performance of the training group relative to the control group on two aspects of the Porteus Maze Tests; however, Palkes, Stewart, and Freedman (1972) found the effect rather short-lived.

Staats, Staats, Schultz, and Wolf (1962) showed that reinforcers such as tokens could be used to keep four-year-old children at work on a series of somewhat tedious exercises aimed at teaching them to read. A more recent study by Brent and Routh (1978) successfully reduced word recognition errors. Fourth graders with average intellectual ability but poor reading achievement were given two word-recognition lists, the first one as a pretest and the second test under one of three conditions: control; positive reinforcement (one nickel for each word read correctly); and response cost (one of 40 nickels taken back for each error). The controls showed no change; those given positive reinforcers slowed down their time to respond but did not make fewer errors. Only the response-cost subjects showed a true decrease in errors and impulsive reading.

Hopkins, Schutte, and Gorton (1971) studied the effects of access to a playground upon the speed with which first- and second-grade children copied writing assignments from the blackboard. The children worked faster and had fewer errors when given the opportunity to spend time on the playground when finished with their assignments.

Winett and Winkler (1972), in their review of the literature, suggested that behavior modification researchers were much more interested in keeping students silent and immobile than in the quality of their learning experience. They contrasted behavior modification philosophy unfavorably with that of the British open classroom which, among other things, encouraged students to learn at their own pace. O'Leary (1972) replied on behalf of behavior modification researchers that the open classroom might not be the best approach for children with social and/or academic problems.

A summary of programs using token awards reported that, in more than 100 token reinforcement programs in the United States (O'Leary & Drabman, 1971), although those programs had clearly demonstrated their effectiveness, they seemed to have a greater effect on children's social behavior than on their academic performance. It is further reported that the programs sometimes fail, even though the failures are seldom reported in the literature. In addition, particular children seem resistant to their effects, and there is little evidence of long-term effects or generalization across settings.

## PSYCHOANALYTIC PRINCIPLES

Psychoanalytic principles are presented because learning problems may be a result of deep-seated emotional problems. The defenses children use when confronted with failure must be understood when working with a learning-disabled child.

Freud (1953) was probably the first theorist to emphasize the developmental aspects of personality and to stress in particular the decisive role of the early years of infancy and childhood in laying down the basic character structure of the person. In psychoanalysis, Freud reconstructed the past life of a person from evidence furnished by adult recollections. Personality develops, according to Freud, in response to four major sources of tension: physiological growth processes; frustrations; conflicts; and threats. As a direct consequence of increases in tension emanating from these sources, the person is forced to learn new methods of reducing tension. This learning is what is meant by personality development.

The individual learns to resolve her frustrations, conflicts and anxieties through identification and displacement. Identification refers to imitating a model seen as ideal and becoming like that person, while displacement refers to searching for a model substitute when no model is available. The process of displacement is usually unsatisfactory. Identification and displacement are influential in shaping the individual's ego.

Under pressure of extreme anxiety the ego is forced to take measures to relieve the anxiety. These measures are called defense mechanisms. According to Anna Freud (1946), the principal defenses are repression, projection, reaction formation, and regression. These defense mechanisms have two characteristics: they deny, falsify, and distort reality; they operate unconsciously so that the person is not aware of what is taking place.

Thus a new concept, "the unconscious," was first introduced. Freud (1949) formulated the development of the id, ego, and superego as three balancing, interactive forces determining the individual's personality. The model formalized a theoretical dichotomy between a drive system (the id) and an inhibitory system (the ego). The newborn is driven by primary processes and later, with the establishment of the ego, develops secondary processes of thought. The superego, commonly considered the conscience of the individual, is self-observing and self-criticizing. It is shaped by the primitive, critical, and judgmental attitudes of the parents as absorbed and internalized by the child to become part of his inner world. The id is the reservoir of the drives, and the ego is the organization of functions involved in the control of the drives, and in the individual's adaptation to reality. It is the ego which is the modulating force between the id and the superego.

Psychoanalysis is considered a drive-reduction theory. It assumes that each individual seeks and strives toward homeostasis. This attempt to lessen the anxiety and conflict caused by the drives and influenced by the superego is the constant struggle through which the developing ego tries to reach a rational and homeostatic way of dealing with the world: "The model also considers the interrelationships of several other psychological processes including memory, attention, perception, consciousness, censorship and the motivational activation of each of them" (Holzman, 1970, p. 108).

Psychoanalysts depend on the medical disease model and, in particular, the concept of the underlying unitary pathology (e.g., the unconscious conflict) producing a plethora of surface manifestations or symptoms (Werry & Wollersheim, 1967). However, the major concern in psychoanalysis is not with the symptoms but with the preexisting states that caused the symptomatology. Whereas the behaviorists see the essential characteristics of learning as the potency of environmental events or external stimuli in eliciting responses from a helpless or passive organism, the psychoanalytic therapist views the problem as stemming from an interaction of biological and environmental factors in the early years of life. To change behavior, according to this theory, requires a lengthy recapitulation of the early years of life.

## Research in Psychoanalytic Theory

Contemporary American psychology as a whole has come to regard the experimental method as a scientific technique for approximating truth. Psychoanalysis, clinical in its methods, is not experimental and to that extent may be out of step with portions of the American psychological and educational community. Yet only in a restricted view would science be limited in its techniques to those of the experimental method. Manipulation and control of variables are not the only scientific procedures. The controlled observation of phenomena, with provision for reflecting either the observations or the statement linking them, claims equal status as a scientific method. Psychoanalysis, which begins with observations of human behavior, proceeds from just such an empirical base. The constant revision of theories in keeping with new observations demonstrates the strength of the method (Holzman, 1970).

Freud (1953) himself, in reporting his case studies, was an astute observer of behavior. Much of his formulation is based on the results of his treatment of neurotic patients. Psychoanalysis has contributed to an understanding of hitherto unexplored psychopathological states and certain aspects of human behavior such as unconscious mental processes and motivational structures. Anna Freud is probably the most influential clinical educator and proponent of the psychoanalytic approach to the teaching and learning of children. She believes that growth takes place along three independent lines: body independence, social development, and work-play. Where development is uneven, growth becomes distorted, and it is possible for learning disabilities to result.

Gerald Pearson (1952), following a psychoanalytic line, suggests that learning disorders may manifest themselves in the inability to take in information as a result of any one of many factors, including anxiety, lack of trust, fearfulness of what one can learn, repression, and denial. If one believes in this theory, the treatment of the "learning-disabled child" would involve drive reduction and play therapy to lessen the regressive and repressive tendencies. One would have to come to grips with whatever defense system the child had acquired, which instead of helping the situation tended to hinder it. Unfortunately, there is little research that supports or denies this principle. However, there are programs that use this approach, e.g., the Family Therapy Institute in Philadelphia (Minuchin, 1965), as well as many therapeutic nursery programs.

## THE HOLISTIC-DYNAMIC THEORY: SELF-ACTUALIZATION

Abraham Maslow (1954) aligned himself closely with an organismic or, as he calls it, a holistic-dynamic point of view. He felt that psychology had dwelled more upon man's frailties than upon his strengths. He wanted to think of man making desperate attempts to gain pleasure and happiness, rather than the psychoanalytic view of man struggling to avoid pain. Maslow (1954) writes as follows:

> Now let me try to present briefly and at first dogmatically the essence of this newly developing conception of the psychiatrically healthy man. First of all and most important of all is the strong belief that man has an essential nature of his own, some skeleton of psychological structure that may be treated and discussed analogously with his physical structure, that he has needs, capacities and tendencies that are genetically-based, some of which are characteristic of the whole human species, cutting across all cultural lines, and some of which are unique to the individual.

These needs are on their face good or neutral rather than evil. Second, there is involved the conception that full healthy and normal and desirable development consists in actualizing this nature, in fulfilling these potentialities, and in developing into maturity along the lines that this hidden, covert, dimly seen essential nature dictates, growing from within rather than being shaped from without. . . . Third, it is now seen clearly that psychopathology in general results from the denial or the frustration or the twisting of man's essential nature. . . . What is psychotherapy?. . . . Any means of any kind that helps to restore the person to the path of self-actualization and of development along the lines that his inner nature dictates. (pp. 340-341)

Maslow, as one can see, addresses the goodness in man. When man becomes neurotic or miserable it is because the environment has made him so through ignorance and/or social pathology. Maslow asks that the environment be set aside and not interfere with man's self-actualization. Aggression and destructiveness are not indigenous to man and only develop when man's inner nature is twisted or denied or frustrated. As soon as the frustration is removed, aggression will disappear.

This self-actualization theory assumes that needs are arranged along a hierarchy of priority or potency as follows (from most to least potent): physiological needs such as hunger and thirst; safety needs; needs for belonging and love; esteem needs; need for self-actualization; cognitive needs, such as a thirst for knowledge; and, finally, aesthetic needs. According to Maslow, man will only become antisocial when society denies him the fulfillment of his inborn needs.

Maslow wanted psychologists to study self-actualizing personalities—healthy people. He made an intensive and far-reaching investigation of a group of self-actualizing individuals that included Eleanor Roosevelt and Albert Einstein. They were investigated clinically to see what characteristics distinguished them from the ordinary run of people. He discovered that the self-actualizing person has these distinguishing features:

1) realistically oriented;
2) accepts him/herself, other people, and the natural world for what it represents;

3) spontaneous;
4) problem-centered rather than self-centered;
5) a private person with an air of detachment;
6) autonomous and independent;
7) a fresh appreciation of people;
8) profound spiritual or mystical experiences, not necessarily religious;
9) identifies with mankind;
10) profound and deeply emotional intimate experiences;
11) democratic values and attitudes;
12) not confused between means and ends;
13) a sense of humor which is philosophical not hostile;
14) creativity;
15) nonconformance to culture.

The self-actualizing approach has many followers in education. The principle that all people want to succeed and will strive toward success can be seen in the motivation of many handicapped children who continually work and achieve. For those children who have given up the fight, the treatment would involve reestablishing the kind of important relationship that conveys once again that success can be around the corner but that it will take enormous energy and hard work. Adults who have had handicaps and have overcome them to lead successful lives often attribute their success, in part, to a relationship with some one person in their early years who inspired them and turned the tide for them.

## THE DEVELOPMENTAL-INTERACTION THEORY

This theory has direct relevance to learning and was developed by Barbara Biber (1955) at the Bank Street College of Education. It is based on the premise that the cognitive and affective structures which should be nourished emerge naturally from the interaction between the child and her environment under conditions where such interaction is fostered, such as in school programs that enhance both the affective and cognitive domains. The emphasis in this theory is on the interaction of the cognitive and affective systems. The distinctive features of this approach are described by Shapiro and Biber (1973):

> Developmental refers to the emphasis on identifiable patterns of growth and modes of perceiving and responding which are characterized by increasing differentiation and progressive integration as a function of chronological age. Interaction refers, first, to the emphasis of the child's interaction with the environment—adults, other children, and the material world—and second, to the interaction between cognitive and affective spheres of development. The developmental-interaction formulation stresses the nature of the environment as much as it does the patterns of the responding child. (p. 688)

This approach flows from three main sources:

1) the dynamic psychology of Freud and his followers, especially those who have been concerned with the development of autonomous ego responses, e.g., Anna Freud (1963), Erikson (1963), Hartman (1950), and Rapaport (1960);
2) the gestalt and developmental psychologists who have been primarily concerned with cognitive development, like Wertheimer (1944), Werner (1948), and Piaget (1961); and
3) the educational theorists and practitioners who have developed a functional and/or psychodynamic approach of their own, as for example John Dewey (1963), Harriet Johnson (1928), and Lucy Sprague Mitchell (1950).

When psychological theories are put to practical use and the lives of children shaped by their application, it becomes important to make assumptions explicit and specify the psychological processes being fostered. It is a basic tenet of the developmental-interaction approach that the growth of cognitive functions—acquiring and ordering information, judging, reasoning, problem-solving, using systems of symbols—cannot be separated from the growth of personal and interpersonal processes—the development of self-esteem and a sense of identity, internalization of impulse control, capacity for autonomous response, and relatedness to other people. The interdependence of these developmental processes is the sine qua non of the developmental-interaction approach.

## CONTRASTING INSTRUCTIONAL THEORIES BASED ON DIFFERING PHILOSOPHIES

In the late 1950s and early 1960s, Bruner (1966) attempted to contrast the nature of a theory of instruction with a theory of learning. He stated that, while a theory of learning is descriptive, a theory of instruction is prescriptive in the sense that it sets forth the rules specifying the most effective ways to achieve knowledge or mastery of skills. According to Bruner, a theory of learning describes the conditions under which competence is acquired. A theory of instruction sets up criteria of performance and then specifies the conditions required for meeting them. Skinner (1968), on the other hand, in the course of his interest in the technology of teaching, made the development of procedures for prescribing conditions for learning almost indistinguishable from a theoretical description of learning. Piaget (1961), however, continued to make the point that children pass through normative stages of cognitive development. He repeatedly insisted that, specific training not withstanding, children reach these stages of development with normal maturation of their specific constitutional endowments, providing that they have been exposed to the normal experiences of childhood.

It becomes immediately evident that there is a dichotomy between the Skinnerian and Piagetian approach which needs careful consideration, and that the flow of research about these diverse theoretical positions needs to be fed directly to the teacher-practitioner. It also may be possible that both Piaget and Skinner have something to offer for very different situations, and this too requires specific analysis.

John Dewey, in his presidential address before the American Psychological Association (1899), expressed concern about developing a linking science between psychological theory and practical use. The decisive matter, according to Dewey, was the extent to which the ideas of the theorist actually projected themselves into the consciousness of the practitioner. It is the participation by the practical man in the theory, through the agency of the linking science, that determines at once effectiveness of the work done and what he calls "the moral freedom and personal development" of the one engaged in it. It is the teacher's inability to regard, upon occasion, both himself and the child as objects working upon each other in specific ways. This sometimes leads to the teacher's use of purely arbitrary measures. He may tend, then, to fall back upon mere routine traditions of school teaching or to fly to the latest fad of pedagogues.

In the past teachers have been confused or frustrated by diagnostic information that failed to translate into effective instruction. In their desperation they have grabbed at gimmicks and commercially made materials, failing to realize that what may be significant is what happens between two people, how well they understand the cognitive processes of the learner, how flexible they can be in adjusting to the needs of the child, and how well they can create new tasks through which students may achieve success. If there is a concern with the development of a link between research and practical application, one must consider those theorists who have tried to create that link. Certainly B. F. Skinner (1968) is one example of a theorist who tried to work through this linking structure via programmed learning and teaching machines.

## TAXONOMIES

Bloom (1956) identified taxonomies in the cognitive, affective, and psychomotor domains. Learning was assumed to occur in an orderly sequence from the simple to the complex. Gagne's (1971) learning hierarchy attempted to classify several kinds of learning postulates by classical and contemporary psychologists (including Pavlov, Watson, Hull, Skinner, Osgood, Bruner, Ausubel). Unfortunately, taxonomies failed to provide adequate foundations for generating instructional programming based on theoretical hierarchies. Lacking was the cognitive-affective integration of different experiences with instructional programming (White, 1973).

Theorists like Piaget (1961) and Hunt (1969) have focused on the important match between experiential variables and the child's present developmental level—the closer the match, the more probable the desired behavioral change. Developmental readiness (Bloom, 1964) is seen as the child's internal readiness to benefit and learn from experience. Developmental pressure is seen as just the right amount of pressure to exert beyond the child's current level of functioning and what is needed for her to move to the next step of cognitive integration. As a result of this concept, one group of educators em-

phasized homogenous grouping and the use of self-instructional programmed workbooks, while another group deemphasized structure
and sequencing, encouraging instead many varied experiences to act
as catalysts for learning which, it was believed, would evolve as a
natural consequence.

## TASK ANALYSIS

Task analysis was considered next in the development of individualized instruction. Task analysis requires an intuitive practical base
involving trial and error experimentation, flexibility of instruction
based on observation, and a critical and frequent use of individualized,
informal evaluation which is constantly checking hypotheses. The task
analysis approach has much to offer, but sometimes special educators
have a tendency to focus on immediate, short-term programming. In
conjunction with task analysis, new criterion-referenced assessment
techniques were developed which, according to their developers, had
universal appeal as well as instructional legitimacy for handicapped
populations. Criterion-referenced assessment has value but is limited
because it pays more attention to product than process. Nevertheless,
the value of task analysis is that it allows more understanding of what
is asked and can lead to an understanding of the process used by each
individual. This encourages long-range planning of strategies because
of the knowledge learned from studying process.

## DIAGNOSTIC-PRESCRIPTIVE MODEL

Just as theorists have developed theories of learning and instruction,
many special educators have presented models for teaching exceptional
children. One attempt to bring a greater degree of coordination and
integration to the process of individualization has been the diagnostic-
prescriptive model. This model has its roots in systems theory and
is based on behavioral philosophy. Most of the theories prescribe
linear sequences, a systematic, hierarchical approach to learning
(Adelman, 1971; Cartwright & Ysseldyke, 1973; Lerner, 1973; Minskoff, 1973), and imply direct applicability in the classroom. They
incorporate task analysis, the use of behavioral objectives, and cri-

terion-referenced testing in a total package defining individualized instruction.

The diagnostic-prescriptive model infers that one can pinpoint diagnosis, indicate exactly where a child falls along a linear line of achievement, and proceed to teach in a linear fashion. It is a hierarchical conception of the learning process which, according to some theorists, leads to higher and higher orders of learning. It further suggests that one can use the paradigm of pretest, instruct, and posttest. Evaluation in this diagnostic-prescriptive model assumes the child is either correct or incorrect, with the focus on the outcome (product), not on the differing ways (process) a child may have used to arrive at a specific outcome. In this model, clinical diagnosis is generally separated from educational treatment. Typically several people perform the diagnosis and then prescribe activities that form the basis of a treatment plan. The diagnosticians in this model are responsible for recommending or designing appropriate educational environments and procedures for each child based on the child's strengths and weaknesses. This sometimes produces two bodies of information in which remedial procedures are limited to the information gathered from a particular testing experience.

Mann (1973) has indicated that the diagnostic-prescriptive methodology that programs children based on the strengths and weaknesses of their performance on particular tests (Frostig, 1961; ITPA, 1961) has little validity. Children who have performed poorly on a subtest of the ITPA or Frostig are often able to do tasks of a similar nature and, in reverse, children may have done well on other subtests and yet seem unable to translate that knowledge to a particular classroom task.

In addition, the prescription that results from this evaluation may not consider the following essential factors:

1) critical contextual variables present in the classroom which directly affect the child's ability to learn (grouping policies, methodology used, multisensory nature of presentation, pace, number of repetitions, number of children, levels of other children, noise, evaluation tools used, etc.);
2) semantic differences in language used in presenting the prescription;

3) differences in experiential level of evaluator and teacher, involving ways the teacher puts the prescription into operation; and

4) differences in interaction between child and evaluator as compared to child and teacher.

Ysseldyke (1973) suggests "there is little support for claims that instruction can be differentiated on the basis of diagnostic strengths and weaknesses." He points out that the match between a child's level of functioning and the instruction selected is seldom realized because procedures used for evaluation (Frostig, 1961; Early Identification Scales [Sapir & Wilson, 1978]; ITPA, 1961) lack the sensitivity to reflect the dynamic nature of the child-teacher-instruction interaction. He advocates two alternatives: develop more reliable assessment instruments with demonstrated validity, or stop the use of standardized tests and focus on the *systematic collection of observational data.*

## ENVIRONMENTAL INTERVENTION THROUGH CONTROL OF STIMULATION

Theories have been put forward based on the "over and under-stimulation" hypothesis. Strauss and Lehtinen (1947) viewed the brain-injured child as excessively distractible and recommended that all extraneous stimulation be removed from the classroom or child's room. They further suggested that the child be given an individual study carrel. Cruickshank, Bentzen, Ratzburg, & Tannhauser (1961) designed a complete educational program for brain-injured children based on those principles. After a one-year longitudinal study to test its effectiveness, no significant differences were found. Sapir (1971) found in her research that the planning and organization of the stimuli prepare the children for further group activity and are more effective than isolating a child in a carrel. For example, using one sharply focused stimulus at first and then gradually embedding the stimulus in busier fields prepares the child to cope with the busy auditory and visual stimuli in his environment. Zentall (1975) has theorized that hyperactive behavior might be an attempt by an under-aroused child to optimize stimulation rather than a reaction to over-stimulation.

Forehand and Baumeister (1970) found that both auditory and visual stimulation had the effect of reducing the activity of severely retarded, institutionalized subjects.

## ECOLOGICAL MODEL

Because learning-disabled children experience their environment differently than normal children, this model is considered here. The ecological model integrates the individual and his environment (Carroll, 1974; Posner, 1974). Here contextual, interpersonal, and intrapersonal characteristics are identified and classified as a means of systematically assessing their effects on rate and style of learning. Diagnosis based on direct observation within and outside the classroom would involve identification, classification, and synthesis of conditions under which the child can and cannot learn (Semmel, 1974). Such diagnostic analysis might be productive both from an instructional and a research perspective: Instructional results and benefits may be quickly realized; relevance and validity of observational data may become self-evident; and the teacher might become the recipient of immediately useful information from both a classroom and research perspective. It might enable the teacher, with time, to identify specific learning styles so that optimal instructional patterns can emerge. This approach requires the teacher to provide individualized instruction in a single sequence or group of sequences. The teacher identifies and decides which unit is a logical next step in programming for a specific child. Each unit may obtain one or several objectives and the teacher identifies how much and what kind of information the child must acquire to reach criterion. In this approach, there is a test-operate (in case the child needs more information), a test sequence and, if the objective is reached, an exit (to terminate instruction).

The responses the child makes provide the teacher with needed data with which to make instructional adjustments. These changes may be qualitative and/or quantitative and reflect interactions among variables. The interrelationships among learner, teacher, and context might suggest program changes and permit inferences about underlying psychological process such as perception and conceptualization. With this approach, it may be possible that the dynamic, continuous nature of learning is more likely recognized and, more importantly, the probability of long-range, individualized programming is enhanced.

## DECISION-MAKING MODEL

Shavelson (1975) has proposed a decision-making model which has interesting implications. This model requires the teacher to be aware of the dynamic interactions among cognition, affect, and the environment. It encourages the teacher to generate a dynamic pattern of conditions under which a child learns best. The choice the teacher makes as to what strategy to use with the child is based on the teacher's personal perception of relevant and functional categories. The teacher, in this model, is urged to attend to the child's varying moods and cognitive style for different tasks. This procedure may lead to continuous reevaluation of options available to the teacher based upon his subjective perceptions of changes in the child. The goal would be for the teacher to anticipate instructional needs rather than react to instructional failure.

## THE CLINICAL DIAGNOSTIC TEACHING MODEL

This model attempts to integrate the position of other approaches with basic child developmental theory (Sapir & Nitzburg, 1973). It is based on the developmental-interaction approach. The model encourages observational tools as diagnostic procedure, but this time the observations are structured by theories of child development (Chess, 1967; Chomsky, 1973; Erikson, 1963; A. Freud, 1963; Hebb, 1949; Luria, 1961; Piaget, 1961; Werner, 1948). It recognizes that children who have experienced failure for long periods of time may need reinforcement. It understands that teachers need to know how to analyze curriculum and perform task analysis. This model encourages the teacher to integrate knowledge of social, temperamental, emotional, and cognitive development, and it enables the teacher to make the best possible decisions regarding treatment for each individual, based on significant knowledge and observations. The therapist, teacher, and diagnostician become one.

The model is based on the belief that children grow and function as total beings with emotional, social, physical, and intellectual dimensions interacting with each other and with the human and physical environments which surround them. Learning is viewed as part of the maturation process, which depends on constant, sensitive, reciprocal interaction between adult and child. In the introduction to their book, Sapir and Nitzburg (1973) state the need to relate knowledge about normal development to children with learning disorders:

> . . . Important concepts about cognitive, social and emotional growth need to be considered. At a conference on "The Roots of Excellence," Barbara Biber stated that: ". . . there is a very fundamental relation between learning and personality development. The two interact in what we speak of as a 'circular process.' According to Dr. Biber, mastery of symbol systems (letters, words, numbers), reasoning, judging, problem-solving, acquiring and organizing information and all such intellectual functions are fed by and feed into varied aspects of the personality for relatedness, autonomy, creativity and integration. The school has a special area of influence for healthy personality because it can contribute to the development of the ego strength. How a child is taught affects his image of himself, which in turn influences what he will dare and care to learn. The challenge is to provide opportunities that will make the most of this circular growth process toward greater learning powers and inner strength. (pp. xv-xvi)

The clinical diagnostic treatment model views the child as a growing, dynamic being, not in a static state, and the teaching or intervention process must respond accordingly as a dynamic, changing process. It assumes that every child can and does learn.

CHAPTER 3

# The Clinical Teaching Model: Philosophical Basis

The basic philosophy of the Clinical Teaching Model is to build on an "island of health." It is to understand the complexity of organization, not only which factors play a determining role in the course of the individual's growth, but also *how* these factors interact to influence that course. The goal is to maximize positive growth and development of a learning-disabled child who can cope with his problem.

With this model, behavior is viewed as simultaneously determined by the inborn structure, past experiences, and the particular present situation. Ideas tend to be incorporated into a complex system of thought schemata. The way one organizes the environment to allow for certain appropriate experiences will determine whether the child can build a cognitive structure on which he can achieve age-appropriate intellectual mastery. An optimal environment should provide the structure that will enable children to develop feelings of competence and self-esteem as they master cognitive and social skills necessary to their functioning (Sapir, 1980). To do this, children must perceive their competence as valid and must be able to use it in an effective interaction with people and work. Furthermore, the ingredients of ego strength and the associated competence fostered by the school must be appropriate to the child's developmental stage. Writing about the developmental-interaction approach, Shapiro and Biber (1973) state,

> . . . the school also promotes the integration of functions, rather than, as is more often the case, the compartmentalization of functions. Thus, the school supports (with this approach) the integration of thought and feeling, thought and action, the subjective and the objective, self-feeling and empathy with others, original and conventional forms of communication, spontaneous and ritualized forms of responses. . . . Generally stated, it is the goal of the school to minimize the gap between capacity and performance by providing an environment that allows and encourages children to do what they are capable of. . . . It is a basic tenet of the Developmental Interaction approach that the growth of cognitive functions—acquiring and ordering information, judging, reasoning, problem solving, using systems of symbols—cannot be separated from the growth of personal and interpersonal processes—the development of self-esteem and a sense of identity, internalization of impulse control, capacity for autonomous response, relatedness to other people. . . . Educational goals are conceived in terms of developmental processes, not concrete achievements. (p. 690)

## THE INTEGRATED APPROACH

These goals can be translated into an effective integrated program for exceptional youngsters. White's (1959) definition of "competence" is central to its goals. "Competence" is defined as the totality of being—a feeling that one has been able to master certain skills which will promote cognitive power and intellectual mastery, nurture self-esteem and understanding, encourage interaction with people, and strengthen the commitment to and pleasure in work and learning. Sapir and Nitzburg (1973) stated that children are developing organisms, constantly changing. Many current approaches fragment the understanding and treatment of the child. They do not allow for treatment on all levels simultaneously—cognitive, emotional, and experiential. The tendency is to do visual-perceptual training in one place with one person, reading instruction with another, language training with a third, and psychotherapy detached from the learning environment with a fourth. It is not possible to isolate the learning environment from every other aspect of the growing child. Needed are "child specialists" who understand therapeutic procedures within a framework of diagnostic teaching, who understand the child's feelings as well as her thinking processes. They need to develop skills to enable them to analyze a cognitive task, determine a child's learning style, and relate it to the child's personality and temperament. The Clinical Teaching Model is an attempt to "reintegrate" the child and to establish the view that all children, including those in trouble, have normal developing processes.

Such a program emphasizes:

1) *Listening, understanding,* and *sharing* with the child how she feels and where she is cognitively, emotionally, and socially.
2) *Clinical-diagnostic* teaching, which is predicated on the principle that diagnosis proceeds from observing the child's attempts to solve tasks, being able to analyze the tasks in terms of what processes are involved, and discovering with the child those parts of the task in which the child can be successful and those parts that are causing problems. The goal is a precise match between the cognitive style of the learner, the cognitive demands of the task, and the style of the therapist.
3) *Working with the child's strengths,* providing success, and building self-esteem that will allow for the development of more pleasure, motivation, and persistence.
4) Through discussions, helping children discover their *compensatory mechanisms,* those mechanisms which will enable them to proceed more successfully through cognitive developmental stages.
5) Rearranging the child's environment at home and school so that it provides *support systems,* to help her with the numerous life experiences with which she will continue to have diffi-

culty. This requires counseling with parents and cooperation with teachers.

The philosophy embodied here is an eclectic one which assumes that growth in one area affects growth in all areas. Attitudes, feeling tone, and cognitive development are considered to foster a sense of competence.

Skills need to be taught as they are needed experientially, in an integrated way so that reading, and writing, as well as perceptual and conceptual skills, can be seen as a unified whole. Emphasis needs to be placed on a schemata that fosters thinking processes and encourages the development of strategies that will be effective, regardless of the circumstances. An example of such a unified approach might be the following. Children become interested in alphabet letters. They can be encouraged to sort them, hear similarities and differences, match them, think of children's names and how they write them. Where do the letters go and why? Which children's names begin the same way and why? Listen to sounds about them; reproduce the sounds. Do they sound like any letter sounds? What shapes have meanings to them? Do the letters remind them of something? What concrete object might they think of when they think of a letter? What words have special meaning for them? Do they want to know what they look like? Do they want to put something down with letters (maybe from one of their pictures) so that others can know what they are thinking?

With learning-disabled children, definitions and descriptions are many and varied because no learning-disabled child is like another. Symptoms occur in clusters and vary from child to child. Specific learning disability is a variable clinical syndrome that changes with age. In the normal child, there are primary modes of processing at different ages and stages. As soon as competence is reached at one stage, there is a shift of function to another (Piaget, 1962).

Where there is a deficit at a lower order of thinking or perceiving, it is not possible to retrace one's steps and retrain the individual as though she were back at the younger stage of development. When dealing with a multilevel development of great complexity, such simplistic thinking is often ineffective. A child of 12 who has a visual-perceptual discrimination problem cannot be taught the same way as the normal child of four or five years. Many of the current programs do not account for this difference. In no way does this imply that the child does not have to be taught. The mere presentation of an interesting worksheet or exercise is not necessarily teaching. New experiences must be provided, carefully timed and paced at the child's level. Many exceptional children become very frustrated and overwhelmed with the introduction of new material. Developmental pressure describes the educational task of providing a balance between experiences that help consolidate the child's understanding and those that provide desirable, growth-inducing challenge.

The Clinical Teaching Model implies a linking of treatment and diagnosis so that the continually emerging patterns of the child lead to the refinement and revision of strategies. It believes that professionals working together from many disciplines can share their expertise and form a common body of knowledge and skill, as well as a communication system that can provide better service to the children. It has a commitment that only a totally integrated intervention program assists the child to become independent of her handicaps and allows for her natural compensatory mechanisms to emerge.

Many physicians, psychologists, and other professionals have difficulty making a differential diagnosis because of the complexity of the problem, resulting in a delay of aid until it is much too late to help. The child feels that something is wrong but does not understand the nature of the problem. Children usually are not able to express either their feelings or needs to those who could possible help them. Often children see a problem as unique to them and therefore may fear that others will discover their secret. Children may feel certain that many people know their problem but try to ignore them. "Why?", they ask themselves, and no one answers. Ironically, most of these youngsters with specific learning disability are intellectually competent and with help can become quite successful in their life's work. Often with skilled and compassionate handling at home and in school, they may have the opportunity to overcome their handicaps (Sapir & Wilson, 1978).

The goal of an integrated treatment program is to develop children who can become adaptable, coping, competent people with educational and social skills that enable them to learn and function effectively in normal settings. One of the most important facets of the success of such a program is the child-teacher interaction and the attributes the teacher must have in order to provide successful experiences for children. The teacher must be sensitive and perceptive, have fine observational and decision-making skills, allow for the child's natural exploration of ways to succeed, and have knowledge of task analysis, information processing systems, and child development theories. The teacher must also provide the back-up support systems (both cognitive and emotional) that will allow the child to proceed. The teacher has to be able to translate for the child, in simple language, the process the child uses that is successful so that the strategies that work for her can be encouraged and translated to others (family, friends, teachers). They too can support and encourage the successful strategies.

This Clinical Teaching Model represents a belief that learning-disabled children can and do learn; that they have their own strengths and compensatory mechanisms; that these compensatory mechanisms can be encouraged to emerge through a support system of teachers, resource people, parents, and peers; that these support people must be committed to the view of the child as a competent person. Then, and only then, will cognitive strategies and techniques become transferable and integrated into more effective performance.

Weil (1970) stated that no matter at what age we see a child first, it is helpful to try to reconstruct the interaction of forces that brought about the clinical picture. About children with specific learning disabilities, we might speculate: What was the original makeup of the children? What is the range of the emotional endowment, from very warm, outgoing, and reachable to more withdrawn and introverted? What would these children have been without the dysfunction and/or if they had grown up in a different, better environment? And with such children there is a more specific question: How much have the inherent experiences of frustration and failure contributed, and how much have environmental misunderstanding, pressure, disappointment, and lack of structure contributed to the final clinical picture? Gardner (1971) makes a plea that we understand the brain-damaged child as a "battered hero of evolution" (p. 123) and regard with awe her continuing attempts to adapt in the face of staggering difficulties.

Unitary study is needed of the child, her environment, and the transactions occurring in the child's total life space. If developmental processes are to be understood, it will not be through continuous assessment of the child alone but through a continuous assessment of the transactions between children and their environment to determine how these transactions facilitate or hinder adaptive integration as both children and their surroundings change and evolve (Sameroff & Chandler, 1973).

Glaser (1972) has recommended a complete shift of emphasis from input-output variables to process-related ones. He analyzed what the child was able to do, the point of failure, and how to cue for success. This required the integration of theories of child development with information-processing knowledge and task analysis. His emphasis was to foster "learning to learn" skills; to recognize that basic strategies can be developed with the child; to design flexible instructional sequences in which the entry point in one sequence is determined by the capability of the child. Glaser's approach recognizes that with sufficient time and optimal circumstances all children are capable of learning. Underachievement is no longer viewed as solely a result of some inadequacy within the child, but may instead reflect the inadequacy of the interactive process between learner characteristics, teachers' styles, and variables within the instructional system. Although attempts may be made to individualize important concepts about the child's information-processing system, this must be integrated with knowledge of the steps required to succeed in a task. Lastly, the relationship between adult and child, and the reciprocal way they communicate verbal or nonverbal positive messages are important prerequisites to the learning.

Doris Johnson, speaking at the American Psychological Association Meeting (1976), stated that there can be no simple response or treatment program for this learning-disabled population because of the variability and complexity of their problems. She said that these children need the following: 1) an expectation that they will learn; 2) an adjustment to goals; 3) appropriate placement; 4) tutoring in specific school subjects; and 5) teaching to their strengths as well as working with their deficits. She recommended an exploration of the individual modes of input to facilitate change. In order to help the child learn, it is usually necessary to break down complex tasks into subsystems and to create end products that will be satisfying to the child.

## EDUCATIONAL PROGRAMS

The philosophical and methodological base of the Clinical Teaching Model considers growth as an integration of social, cognitive, and emotional development. Education means learning for life. The curriculum for learning-disabled children must provide an organizational structure that allows for the expression of thoughts and feelings about a large variety of experiences and permits children to discover their own learning processes. The strength gained will help children to share with parents and teachers those things that they can do that will help them learn. The planned educational intervention uses a diagnostic-teaching paradigm with continual communication with children, teachers, and parents.

This model is complex and requires commitment and dedication of professionals, but it is one which provides many challenges and satisfactions. It involves retraining and reorientation of teaching personnel. This is best accomplished right on the job by having a resource person (regardless of discipline in which trained) who can encourage, support, make suggestions, be patient but persevering, demonstrate, and be generally knowledgeable, sensitive, and perceptive to the needs of teachers and children. Change is slow and takes effort. It is far easier to follow what someone tells us to do than to be a keen observer, task-analyzer, decision-maker, and curriculum-developer. But given time to explore, teachers with the help of supportive resource personnel will become autonomous, capable, and responsible for the individual needs of each of their learning-disabled children.

At the very least, teachers should be allowed to develop their own tools for studying children. If they use tests or developmental scales and if they can understand that tasks, tests, or scales are only as good as the observations they elicit, they will then evolve a scientific method of making hunches (hypotheses), testing them out, and drawing conclusions regarding their validity. Such types of teacher training develop creative, thinking, responsible, and accountable personnel who will be able eventually to teach children and take leadership in the training of others.

The teacher who puts into operation a set of linear, sequential steps that is prescribed for a child will forever need to have others direct her efforts. It is far more effective in a school to create teams of teachers to share ideas, study problems, suggest ways to solve them, and help each other become more effective. It is usually helpful to plan the teams in such a way that within each there is one leader and a complement of skills amongst the others in the team. Essential to the team effectiveness is the inclusion of a child specialist who can act as a resource and support person for teachers and children.

Many educational principles have been stated that are important for all children; for the learning-disabled child they become even more critical. In general education, classes in the public schools give lip service to individualization and respect for the child. But we also observe that those children who do not fit into the lockstep of the curriculum are labeled "a problem." There is a mechanistic approach which makes it mandatory that children enter school at a certain age. This approach assumes that all children are ready at the same time and that, if they are not, schools can provide individual programs that will enable the child to succeed. Much of this is a myth. In general education, we now hear terms like "open classrooms," "team teaching," and "non-grading," all of which in principle would be excellent for all children and in particular would provide a framework in which learning-disabled children could find a niche of meaningful and individual activity that would encourage the development of skills in all areas. In reality, the terms are misunderstood. With the best of intentions, either children are left to flounder on their own, or in some cases non-grading becomes departmentalization, which may compartmentalize the child and increases her sense of failure.

An important organizational issue which is presently being argued concerns special classes vs. mainstreaming. Modern thought favors mainstreaming but, as always in the acceptance of any educational "solution," there are concomitant dangers in the loss of options for different children. We would all favor the intent of the new law with its emphasis on "the least restrictive environment." To have special education be an integrated part of the mainstream of all education has always been an inspiration of special educators. The current vigorous emphasis on mainstreaming in the United States is supported as never before by legislation and mandated accountability in the schools. The mainstreaming of children can be satisfactory only if it is accompanied by genuine acceptance and mutual understanding. This movement, will have achieved its ultimate success when exceptional children will not have to be restored to the mainstream because they will never have been excluded from it.

Narrow, separate specialization in special education preparation is unlikely to promote either successful mainstreaming or effective segregated special education. Special education makes the erroneous assumption that children differ markedly in important attitudes or other attributes that, in turn, indicate different instructional programs for their maximal education. In the extreme cases of psychotic or sensory-impaired children (deaf and blind), it is obvious that adjustments in curricula must be made.

The notion that any specific educational intervention program would be suitable for all learning-disabled children is erroneous. A Frostig (1961) program may help a particular child with a visual motor skill; an Ayres (1965) program might improve the flow of body movement; a program of optometrics might help another child become more visually competent. None is a panacea, and the use of any one is validated only when there is an expressed and specific need for a child. Beyond that, any claim for transferability is questionable. There is little substitute for a well-planned individualized approach, one which teaches through the integration of all areas, focuses on strategies (learning how to learn), and embeds the learning in functional and meaningful life experiences. The child must feel and see the need to know something or do something. It may be difficult for the child, for example, to write a letter, but the teacher can set the stage so that it becomes important enough to enable the child to persevere, regardless of problems and the huge amount of energy expended. The task must be important and worthwhile for the child.

There is a fear that enactment of the new laws may become a way to victimize children by labeling them and adapting programs just for the sake of meeting the government mandates. It has finally been recognized that inappropriate assessment procedures have caused many children who are poor, who are of low social status, or who belong to racial or ethnic minority groups to be labeled retarded, disturbed, or socially maladjusted and placed in special education classes. There is evidence that when these children are mainstreamed the results may be disheartening. It becomes obvious, then, that the success or failure of a program rests on more than methodology or an organizational plan; in part, it depends on the willingness and ability of people to make it work, on the knowledge and skills of the personnel, and on the quality of the child-adult interaction.

Any program has to be assessed on the basis of how well it provides for the children under its care. Is the program honest and respectful of children? Does it provide for a reasonable amount of choices for them? Does it account for their individual needs? Does it provide for pleasure in work and play? Are children provided with experiences in which there are "developmental pressures," but through which they can succeed, learn, and grow in self-esteem and cognitive mastery? Does the program allow for a range of activity for all the children in skills, social participation, and creative arts? Do the children succeed and become competent human beings?

Some suggestions may be helpful in working out a program for learning-disabled children. It is possible to utilize, to a great degree, existing personnel and resources within the school, and to involve regular teachers. This, in effect, would promote the idea that they are capable of providing services for the child within the regular classroom.

It is possible to establish a materials resource center where the regular classroom teacher can be supplied with specialized teaching materials and share ideas without going through the usual administrative delay. A child specialist could be available to provide the *support system* for teachers and children. Such a person can present new ideas and demonstrate new methods to the teachers, as well as provide additional services to the child. To be effective, the child specialist should work with no more than 15 teachers and be responsible for about 350 children, assuming that not more than 10 to 20% of these youngsters will need much special help.

Walzer and Richmond (1973) state:

> We are concerned ultimately with the child's adaptation—his capacity to use to the fullest his internal and external resources in order to function optimally under any circumstances in which he is placed. Successful adaptation is possible only when some degree of homeostasis exists among the many variables considered. With this model, learning can be viewed as a complex, adaptive phenomenon influenced by any or all of the factors presented. Because such a conceptual framework emphasizes the interaction of various factors as they affect learning, it permits

a logical organization of our knowledge in this area in a way that relates the various data within an overall perspective. (pp. 551-552)

The challenges are many. But let us hope they will inspire us to create and adapt effective models, to learn more about ourselves and the children with whom we are working, to keep an open mind to new ideas, to constantly explore, critique and stimulate and, above all, to share with others. Our thoughtfulness, honesty, and concern for the child, our respect for what the child has to tell us, should be our first and most important priority.

# CHAPTER 4

# What We Learn From Normal Child Development in Working With the Learning-Disabled Child

---

The principles of child development are presented here because with the Clinical Teaching Model a knowledge of normal development is vital to the understanding of the learning-disabled child. One must understand normal growth and behavior, because the child with learning problems is normal in many ways. The developmental point of view sees the child as an ever-evolving organism passing through stages, each of which is relevant to earlier and later development (Piaget, 1966). A developmental-interaction theory precludes the separation of affect from cognition, and the separation of the genetically determined constitution of the child from the environmental influences.

The acquisition of developmental milestones will be considered within the framework of a developmental-interaction system. Here, developmental refers to the emphasis on identifiable patterns of growth and modes of perceiving and responding, which are characterized by increasing differentiation and progressive integration as a function of chronological age. Interaction refers first to the child's interaction with his environment and, second, to the interaction between neurological, cognitive, and affective spheres of development.

These maturing systems interact in what we speak of as a "circular process." Mastery of symbol systems (letters, words, and numbers), reasoning, judging, problem-solving, acquiring and organizing information, and all such intellectual functions are fed by and feed into varied aspects of the personality, such as feelings about oneself, identity, potential for relatedness, autonomy, creativity, and integration. The home and school have a special influence on healthy personality because they can contribute to the development of ego strength. How a child is taught affects his image of himself, which in turn influences what he will dare and care to learn. The challenge is to provide opportunities that will make the most of this circular growth process toward greater learning powers and inner strength.

The child is a complex organism with all systems in constant interaction. Stimulation of any kind affects all parts of the organism. Children have biological strengths and weaknesses which interact with their environment, helping or hindering their growth (Sapir & Wilson, 1978). The child needs to develop emotional strength that allows for trust and autonomy, and permits freedom of play and exploration before symbolic knowledge is possible. A problem for a child in one area will hinder, stunt, or skew growth in other areas. Only too often does one see emotionally disturbed youngsters who have distortion of perception and language, and children with central nervous system damage having problems with self-esteem and social development. One can maximize the child's strengths and develop a program that will foster the greatest overall growth.

In the normal child, there are primary modes of processing at different ages and stages. As soon as competence is reached in one stage, there is a shift of function to another. For example, Piaget (1929) distinguishes four major stages in the development of intelligence. The first is the sensory-motor stage, the period before the appearance of language. Second is the period from two to seven years of age, known as the pre-operational period. The period from seven to 12 years of age, a period of concrete operations, is next, and the fourth stage, after 12 years of age, is the period of formal operations.

Kephart (1968), using different terms, discusses the motor stage, in which the child develops the tools for environmental encounters; the motor-perceptual stage, during which perceptual information is matched to the previously developed motor information, which remains the controlling factor; the perceptual-motor stage during which perceptual exploration becomes the dominant mode of operation; the perceptual stage, during which perceptions are manipulated against each other; the perceptual-conceptual stage, during which similarities of perceptions are compared and can be combined into an abstracted concept; the conceptual stage, during which one concept is manipulated against another leading to high verbal ability; and the conceptual-perceptual stage, during which the child depends less on perception as a primary source of information and more on conceptual manipulation of information. At this last stage, perceptions are fit into a conceptual frame of reference—thus, the old adage, "We see not what is there, but what we want to see."

It is a common occurrence that when one examines records of a child diagnosed as learning disabled over a long period of time, one discovers the following pattern: at three, the child may have had speech lags; at seven, the perceptual problem (visual-motor or auditory) may have been primary; at nine, with the shift of function, the syndrome has become more language-oriented and the child has had difficulty in word finding (substituting words within a category such as comb for brush) or word usage (unable to shift the meaning of a word such as hole and whole), or the child has had a syntactical problem of shift to another part of speech (block from a noun to a verb); and at a much later age, the difficulty may have manifested itself in written work, with a disability appearing in writing a sentence or a paragraph in an appropriate syntactical form.

A diagnostician or educator should consider the normal stages of development and look at the degree of deviation from the normal. The dysfunction will be manifested in the primary mode of functioning at that particular time in the child's life and may well disappear as the child moves from one stage to another. This does not necessarily imply a developmental lag or maturational problem, but may be an organic dysfunction. The child may have compensated through another intact mode of performance. Educational intervention that is compensatory in nature (Sapir, 1980) is advocated here.

The Clinical Teaching Model emphasizes the integration and chaining of all maturing systems: physiological, neurological, emotional, and social. These maturing systems interact in what we speak of as a "circular process." Mastery of intellectual functions is fed by and tied into varied aspects of the personality—feelings about one's self, identity, potential for relatedness, autonomy, creativity, and integration. The challenge is to provide opportunities that will make the most of this circular growth process, so that children can achieve greater learning powers and inner strength.

Language development is one of the major contributors to ego strength and readiness for academic learning. A child's language growth is demonstrated by increases in quantity, quality, size of vocabulary, sentence length, and degree of abstraction. It is generally believed that inner language is acquired first, receptive language next, and expressive language last. A child does not first learn words and then meaning. Meaningfulness and experience precede the acquisition of words. Only after he has begun to make sense out of his world does the child begin to understand the words that represent experience. When inner language has been established to a minimal degree, the child begins to comprehend auditory verbal symbols (words). Reciprocal relationships among all aspects of language are evidenced by the fact that, with an increase in receptive language, inner language is also increased. Finally, after minimal inner and receptive language have been established, the child acquires expressive language and begins to talk. As the child speaks, he enhances both receptive and inner language. The "verbal mediator" begins to become a factor in the development of higher-order perception and concept formation. This process of language growth continues throughout life. With new and broader experiences, we add new meanings and new words to our vocabularies. Moreover, with the acquisition of new symbols, the potential for creating new thoughts and ideas is increased.

A disturbance in comprehension will affect expressive language. One can observe children who understand but cannot speak. Expressive language has three components: word retrieval, articulation of words, and the syntax of the language. Consider word retrieval or word naming first. There are those children who can remember words for the purpose of recognition when spoken to but not for spontaneous usage. These children with word-finding difficulties exhibit many word substitutions, hesitancies, and often a large flow of words. When shown a comb, they might say "brush," or "thing," or "you know what it is, you use it on your hair," or "that thing with the points on it." Many children with reading problems manifest word-retrieval problems as well. These are often difficult to detect because such children tend to be very verbose and speak rapidly.

The second component of speech development requires a well-defined motor patterning system so that words can be articulated clearly. Children with problems in this area may be unable to enunciate specific sounds. These must be distinguished from those children with auditory processing problems who tend to mispronounce words or misplace syllables, as when they say "sagetti" instead of "spaghetti," or "aminal" not "animal."

The third facet of expressive language pertains to the syntax of the language: the formulation of sentences and the rules for putting words together to make sense. Examples of difficulty in this area can be heard when a child says, "The dog pulled the wagon with the boy," when his action shows that the boy pulled the dog in the wagon. Some children do not understand that words can be used in many different ways. For example, such a child cannot make the shift from, "I rode down the block," to "I build with blocks," or "I block that pass."

An extension of speaking includes the related symbol system: reading and writing. The developmental sequence begins with auditory verbal comprehension (listening) and progresses to oral expression (speaking), reading, and writing. The normal child first learns auditory language, and later he learns to read and write. He superimposes a visual symbol system on the auditory one. If there is a problem in the auditory-oral communication system, there is bound to be difficulty when one has to learn to read or write. But if the child is successful in his growth patterns, he will have two systems for input (listening and reading) and two systems for output (speaking and writing). A disturbance can occur at any point along this developmental continuum.

One anticipates that sometime in the first year of life most children say their first intelligible word. If that is reinforced by a smile, praise, or pat, the child continues to add to his repertoire. A few months later children are saying many words, and some children go about the house naming things (table, dog, ball) saying action words (play, see, come), and using an occasional quality word (blue, bad). At about 18 months, children are apt to construct two-word utterances, such as "push car." The beginning utterances are not said as communications systems but as reinforcers or stimulants for action. At about three years, children with normal development are so advanced in the construction processes as to produce all the major variables of English simple sentences up to a length of 10 or 11 words.

Theories of child development do not exist in isolation from each other. Rather, they reflect the particular interest and concern of their authors. They contribute to the understanding of the course of growth and therefore help one understand when growth has gone awry. As the child matures, he moves from a state of global perception and reaction to increasing differentiation in a hierarchical fashion (Werner, 1948). As the child learns to differentiate increasingly between himself and other people, he becomes less dominated by the stimulus field around him and more able to define himself. He develops concepts about himself and his world, and in this way achieves freedom to organize and control behavior in himself and in the world around him. Each theory is concerned with ways in which and reasons why the child is able to accomplish this mastery. Some feel that the progression of differentiation and hierarchical integration, and the acquisition of certain skills, such as language, are so steady, so rapid, and so complex that they must be based upon innate qualities of the human species and perhaps proceed in maturational patterns that are age-approximate (Chomsky, 1973). Other theories emphasize other aspects of this process, such as the role of speech in developing the regulation of behavior (Luria, 1961), or the contribution of language along with perception to production of concept formation (Piaget, 1955). Still others deal with the "why" of development—the motivational aspects of the human organization and learning (Hebb, 1949).

Many theorists could have been presented here, but space did not allow. Theorists who have explored how the constitution of the child influences and is influenced by experience, and who support an interaction theory include Josselyn (1948), Anastasi (1958), and Hunt (1961). The notion of imprinting at critical periods of development (Hess, 1959) has led to research in infant stimulation and the development of many early-intervention programs (Bruner, 1969; Deutsch, 1965; Sapir, 1961). It has been discovered that when infants' needs are not met, severe problems result (Spitz, 1946).

The choice of which theorists to present reflects the bias of the author. Nevertheless, this is an attempt to present a balanced view of many basic approaches to growth and development. It concentrates on the embryology of behavior (Gesell, 1929), psychoanalytic treatment (S. Freud, 1949), psychosocial development (Erikson, 1963), motivation (Hebb, 1949), cognition (Piaget, 1955), language development (Luria, 1960; Vygotsky, 1962), plus the integration of these positions (Werner, 1948). The aim of the author is to present an integrated view of maturation and development. The knowledge derived from normal development will help generate a new approach to children with unevenly developed systems.

## THEORIES OF ARNOLD GESELL

Because many learning-disabled children have delay in motor skills, language, and adaptive behavior, the theories of Gesell are presented. His studies of normal and handicapped children, visual and postural development, twins, and handedness are considered classics. He emphasized individual differences in maturational pace. In 1929 he stated,

> Growth is a process so intricate and so sensitive that there must be powerful stabilizing factors, intrinsic rather than extrinsic, which preserve the balance of the total pattern and direction of the growth trend. Maturation is a name for this regulatory mechanism. (p. 318)

Gesell (1929) organized his research into four divisions: behavior-motor, language, adaptive, and personal-social. He never lost sight of the fact that all behavior is integrated, but emphasized how the child's innate forces provide the impetus for potential growth. Gesell wrote at a time when the predominant psychology in the United States was Watsonian, which stressed the environmental influence above all else. To balance this trend, Gesell stressed the significance of genetic structure.

According to Gesell, maturation refers to those phases and products of growth which are chiefly due to innate and indigenous factors. He assembled diverse evidence of behavior maturation based on clinical and experimental observations drawn from the following sources:

1) the development of prehension in the first year of life;
2) the development of correspondence in twins' behavioral patterns;
3) the limitations of training, citing examples of twins where one was trained and the other not;
4) the restrictive influence of physical handicap; and
5) the developmental progression in emotional behavior.

Gesell noted that changes in the first year of life mature with subtle but significant accompanying changes in head and body posture, hand and arm attitude, and associated visual behavior. The refinement of the child's eye-hand behavior (prehension) comes from the progressive acquisition and consolidation of a hierarchy of behavior patterns. In twins, regardless of training, each individual twin reaches the same stage of maturation at about the same time. It appears that there is a constant trend toward change. According to Gesell, the nervous system is remarkably resistant to general adversity, citing resistance to malnutrition as an example.

Gesell (1948) created the Gesell Developmental Scale, which is widely used today and produced new ways of assessing children. Guidelines were given to evaluate normal growth patterns in what he termed the "total complex of ontogenetic development."

## ANNA FREUD'S PSYCHOANALYTIC THEORIES OF CHILDHOOD

Many of the learning-disabled children have difficulty with control of their bodies and/or social relations, as well as with academics. The defenses they use to protect themselves from failure are important to identify when developing treatment strategies.

Anna Freud (1962), in contrast to Gesell, was opposed to basing expectations on a child's chronological age. She urged that we try to understand the child from the child's interpretation of his world, one which depends on the development of his mental organization. Unlike Gesell, Freud emphasized the integration of environmental and maturational factors in personality development. She explored the course of psychoanalytic theory, particularly the development of defense mechanisms, as a way to understand a child's development.

Anna Freud (1963) described the course of growth along three independent lines: 1) body independence; 2) social development; and 3) the dimensions of work-play. Developmental lines, as used by Anna Freud (1963), are "historical realities" which convey a convincing picture of an individual child's personal achievement or of his failures in personality development. She thinks of developmental lines as the tracing from dependency to emotional self-reliance and adult object relationship. To have a harmonious personality there should be corresponding growth in all three areas simultaneously. There are those children who have irregular patterns of growth, where the course of development in one of the three areas might lag behind the others. The amount of disequilibrium created by this irregular growth may comprise variations of normality, but if excessive, may be considered pathological. If, for example, a child loves to work but does not get along with his peers and is alienated, disharmony results. It is always the amount of difference in growth patterns among the three developmental lines that makes the child pathological or just lagging behind in certain areas.

In tracing the child's gradual outgrowth of dependent, irrational, id- and object-determined attitudes to an increasing ego mastery of his internal and external world, there are similar lines of development which can be shown to be valid for almost all areas of the individual's personality (A. Freud, 1963). Such lines, always contributed to from the side of both id and ego development, lead, for example, from the infant's sucking and weaning experiences to the adult's rational rather than emotional attitude to food intake; from cleanliness training enforced on the child by environmental pressure to the adult's more or less ingrained and unshakable bladder and bowel control; from the child's sharing and possession of his body with his mother to the adolescent's claim for independence and self determination in body management; from the young child's egocentric view of the world and his fellow beings to empathy, mutuality, and companionship with his contemporaries; from the first erotic play on his own and his mother's body by the way of transitional object (Winnicott, 1953) to toys, games, hobbies, and finally to work. Anna Freud (1963) states:

> Whatever level has been reached by any given child in any of
> these respects represents the results of interaction between drive

and ego-superego development, and their reaction to environmental influences, i.e., between maturation, adaptation, and structuralization. (p. 247)

Anna Freud (1952), early on in her career, had been a teacher of young children and later, when she worked as an analyst, used her observations of her earlier work with young children. She spent five years teaching elementary school before she began her more intensive psychoanalytical work with children of all ages. She has suggested that it would be better practice for persons working with children, especially teachers, to work with many different age groups. She felt that this would discourage the teachers from making inappropriate generalizations about children who at any given age are in transition. The good teacher, child psychologist, or child specialist sees every phase of childhood in terms of what has gone before and what will come afterwards. They need to see and understand the earlier stages of infancy which have led up to what the child is at the present time.

Anna Freud (1947) was interested in the enormous difference between the evaluation of the child's personality by the school teacher and by the parents. She felt that there were three great dangers for the school teacher. First, working too closely with children fosters a loss of perspective between the child's world and the adult world. The teacher tends to get caught up in the children's lives, loses her adult values, and begins to live in the children's world. Second, the teacher may come to look at childhood stages as valued for themselves, and not as a preparation for the future. The third danger is that the teacher will attach herself to the individual child so much as to think of him as her own. According to Anna Freud (1952), if a teacher sees in the child something that reminds her of her own childhood, she wants to help that child and save it from what she may have experienced. Problems arise when the teacher sees the child as being like her brother or sister with whom she fought constantly, or is reminded of something in her own development which she cannot face. There is a great deal of danger to this personal approach. The teacher's role is not that of a mother-substitute any more than the mother's role is that of a teacher-substitute. There is a difference in a child's attitude toward his mother and his teacher. A child wants to be loved by the mother and does not want to be taught by her. The child's attitude toward the mother is a demanding one based on instinctive wishes. The child's attitude toward the teacher is further removed from drive activity; it is one of willingness to give and take in.

A deeper understanding of personality structure will help all people working with children to avoid a common mistake: namely, to approach children of varying ages in the same manner. At nursery age, one needs to deal directly with the child's instinctive wishes, restricting or deflecting drive activities by means of play material. At school age, one can draw on the ego and its intellectual interests rather than on drive-energy (sublimations). The degree to which drives are still visible at school age varies from child to child. After six years, the most common remnants of past instinctive wishes are greediness, thumb sucking, daydreaming, masturbation, aggressiveness, and showing off. Some children fail to outgrow the need for immediate drive gratification. They do not settle down to school demands but are always searching for immediate satisfaction. They cannot wait or work for their pleasures.

In 1962, speaking before the World Organization for Early Childhood Education in London, Anna Freud said that dealing with the older child, as compared with working with the younger child, requires a turning away from the illogical and irrational thinking of the younger child's need to feel at home in this other country, where logic and reason do not exist, and where one proceeds according to different principles of mental development. When working with parents or teachers, Anna Freud stated that she had always been interested in the many misunderstandings that arise between them and the children. The parent and teachers make arrangements for their children with the best intentions, based on external circumstances. Their insight into the conditions as they perceive them are based on reason and logic. But these may be looked upon by the child in a very different spirit. Namely, they are understood in terms of the child's wishes, fantasies, and fears, and are thereby misunderstood. The detailed characteristics of the world of small children and of the language these youngsters speak need more understanding.

## ERIK H. ERIKSON'S PSYCHOLOGICAL THEORIES

Erikson (1950) formulated the relationship of Freudian psychoanalytic theories to the social milieu in which the growing child lives and learns. His theories state that the healthy adult personality is one in which the person actively masters his environment (emotional, social, and cognitive), shows a certain unity of personality, and is able to perceive the world and himself correctly. This has relevance because the learning-disabled child haas difficulty mastering his environment and experiences many perceptual distortions.

Erikson's formulation of the Eight Ages of Man—Basic Trust vs. Basic Mistrust; Autonomy vs. Shame and Doubt; Initiative vs. Guilt; Industry vs. Inferiority; Identity vs. Identity Confusion; Intimacy and Distantiation vs. Self-Absorption; Generativity vs. Stagnation; and Integrity vs. Despair and Disgust—remains a basic and relevant concept in the field. Erikson views the individual as progressing through these eight ages, each of which presents him with a central problem to resolve. The problem comes from the individual's conflict between his need for a sense of inner sameness and continuity, and his need for belongingness. How the environment supports the child in each stage-determined crisis will affect the direction of his development.

Erickson agreed with Freud's far-reaching discovery that "neurotic conflict is not very different in content from the conflict which every child must live through in his childhood and that every adult carries these conflicts with him in the recesses of his personality" (Erikson, 1950, p. 1).

Erikson presents human growth from the point of view of the inner and outer conflicts which the healthy personality weathers, emerging and reemerging with an increased sense of inner unity, an increase of good judgment, and an increase in the capacity to do well according to the standards of the significant persons in his life. His definition of a healthy personality is one which actively masters the environment, has a unity of personality and is able to perceive the world and himself correctly.

Believing in the "epigenetic principle" Erikson (1950) stated that

anything that grows has a ground plan and that out of this ground plan the parts arise, each part having its time of special ascendancy, until all parts have arisen to form a functioning whole. (p. 3)

The healthy child, given a reasonable amount of guidance, can be trusted to obey inner laws of development, laws which create a succession of potentialities for significant interaction with those who tend him. The interaction, although varying from culture to culture, remains within the proper rate and sequence which govern the growth of a personality as well as the organism. Personality can be said to develop according to predetermined steps in the human organism's readiness to be driven toward, to be aware of, and to interact first with the image of mother and later with mankind.

Erikson is best known for his concept of "identity," linking several disciplines and creating new patterns of thought about development. To him "identity" connoted "both a persistent sameness (self-sameness) and a persistent sharing of some kind of essential character with others" (Coles, 1970). His clinical astuteness has provided a basis for understanding the interaction between individuals and society. He described the identity crisis of adolescence, leading the way to a new dimension of psychiatric thought and enabling others to understand some of the vicissitudes of the antisocial tendencies in adolescence. As a result therapists, teachers, and parents are more likely to give unhappy youths the support and time needed to coordinate their conflicting identifications so that they may emerge intact as adults.

Erikson (1950) has defined growth as a branching process with each stage having roots in the biological and social conflicts caused by the demands of the society. The resolutions of these conflicts are depicted as stages through which the individual passes. The individual does not necessarily resolve the conflict of an earlier stage before moving into the next stage. Each stage comes to its ascendance and meets its crisis. It is this encounter with the resulting crisis which Erikson describes for each stage. He concludes that there is a natural order in which the individual develops, with later developmental stages presuming earlier ones. Each stage is significantly related to all others.

Erikson has organized his psychological stages in the development of personality as follows:

## 1) Basic Trust vs. Mistrust

"I am what I am given" characterizes this stage. The first component of a healthy personality is a sense of trust in an attitude toward oneself and the world derived from the experiences in the first year of life. The extreme of mistrust is seen in those who withdraw into themselves. The general state of trust implies not only that one has learned to rely on the sameness and continuity of the outer providers, but also that one may trust oneself and the capacity of one's own organs to cope with urges and that one is able to consider oneself trustworthy enough so that the providers will not need to be on guard. The establishment of enduring patterns for the balance of basic trust over basic mistrust is the task of maternal care—not the quantity offered but the quality. Mothers create a sense of trust by the sensitivity with which they handle the child's needs and their own firm sense of personal trustworthiness. Parents must have ways of guiding the child by balancing between prohibition and permissiveness. They must also be able to provide the child with the conviction that there is meaning to what his parents are doing.

## 2) Autonomy vs. Shame and Doubt

"I am what I will" represents this period. At this stage, the mutual regulation between adult and child now faces its severest test. With the maturation of the muscle system, the consequent ability or inability to coordinate a number of highly conflicting action patterns such as "holding on" and "letting go," and the enormous value this highly dependent child begins to place on his autonomous will become the setting for the crisis that needs to be resolved. The anal zone lends itself more than any other to the expression of stubborn insistence on conflicting impulses because it contains two contradictory modes which must become alternating, namely retention and elimination. This then sets the stage for the battle for autonomy. If outer control is too rigid, robbing the child of his attempt gradually to control his bowels and other functions willingly and by free choice, the child will be faced with a rebellion and defeat. Powerless in his own body and powerless outside, the child will again be forced to seek satisfaction and control either by "regression or fake progression" (1950, p. 15). For example, the child might return to thumb sucking; become whiny and demanding, become hostile and willful, sometimes using his feces or later obscene words; or he will pretend an autonomy and an ability to do without anybody to lean on. Therefore, this stage is the decisive factor between love and hate, cooperation and willfulness, and the freedom or suppression of self-expression. From a sense of self-control without loss of self-esteem comes a lasting sense of autonomy and pride. From a sense of muscular and anal impotence, of loss of self-control and of parental over-control, comes a lasting sense of shame and doubt. Shame is an infantile emotion and supposes that one is completely exposed and conscious of being looked at. It is expressed in a desire to bury one's face or to sink into the ground.

Another symptom related to this stage is the tendency of the child to overmanipulate himself and develop a precocious conscience. The child becomes obsessed by his own repetitiveness and wants to have everything just so. This infantile obsessiveness manifests itself in dawdling, or by becoming a stickler for certain rituals. The child then learns to gain power over his parents in areas where he could not find mutual regulation with them. The consequence of this for the adult personality can be seen in the classical compulsive character dominated by the wish to get away with things.

If one is firm with and tolerant of the child at this stage, the child will learn to be firm with and tolerant of himself. The child will not only feel pride in being autonomous but will also grant autonomy to others.*

## 3) *Initiative vs. Guilt*

"I am what I imagine I will be" is characteristic of this stage. Having found a firm solution of his problem of autonomy, the child of four or five faces the next crisis. The child has established that he is a person and now wants to know what kind of a person he is going to be. Children want to be like their parents, who appear all powerful and beautiful. The child "identifies" with his parents.

During this stage children learn to locomote and develop a sense of language, both of which permit them to expand their imagination. This, in turn, frightens children because of what they dream and think about. Yet out of all this they develop a realistic sense of ambition and independence.

---

* Author's Note—The struggle for autonomy, when not resolved, sometimes centers around learning problems so that the child can gain power over his parents by not performing academically if this is important to his parents.

This is also the stage of sexual curiosity and an overconcern with sexual matters. It is associated with what Freud has called the "Oedipal complex." The boy child becomes attracted to the mother, the girl child to the father, and they develop a sexual rivalry with the mother or father, whichever is the case. The Oedipal wishes are expressed in the boy's assurance that he will marry the mother and make her proud of him, and the girl's that she will marry the father and take better care of him. The consequence is a deep sense of guilt which seems to imply that the individual has committed crimes and deeds which are impossible to consider.

It is at this stage of initiative that conscience becomes firmly established. The child now feels ashamed of mere thoughts and deeds that nobody has seen.

> Only a combination of early prevention and alleviation of hatred and guilt in the growing being, and the consequent handling of hatred in the free collaboration of people who feel equal in worth although different in kind or function or age, permits a peaceful cultivation of initiative, a truly free sense of enterprise. (Erikson, 1963, p. 31)

## 4) Industry vs. Inferiority

"I am what I learn" characterizes this stage. Children want to watch how things are done and try doing them. This is the time in most societies when children go to school. The school is a world all to itself with its own goals and limitations, achievements and disappointments. During this stage children soon become dissatisfied with the days of make-believe games because they lack the sense of being useful and doing things well. They want to feel industrious, to win recognition by producing things.

The danger at this stage is the development of a sense of inadequacy and inferiority. This is sometimes caused by the unresolved preceding crisis so that the child may want mommy, want to be a baby, or may still be competing with a parent, leading to a sense of guilt.

It is unfortunate but possible for a teacher to instill the idea that the child will never achieve what is expected. This is a very decisive stage socially since industry involves doing things beside and with others, gaining a sense of division of labor and equality of opportunity.

*5) Identity vs. Identity Diffusion*

In this stage, childhood proper comes to an end and youth begins. Adolescence brings with it discontinuity and the questioning of formerly accepted skills and values. This is a period of rapidly growing body and of physical genital maturity. Adolescents are now concerned with consolidating their social roles. In their search for a new sense of continuity, they may have to refight many of the crises of earlier years. The integration now taking place in the form of ego identity is the "inner capital accrued from all those experiences of each successive stage, when successful identification led to a successful alignment of the individual's basic drives with his endowment and his opportunities" (Erikson, 1950, p. 35). Ego synthesis is the accrued confidence that one has the ability to maintain inner sameness and continuity of one meaning for others. Thus self-esteem, confirmed at the end of each major crisis, grows to be a conviction that one is learning effective steps toward a tangible future and that one is developing a defined personality within a social reality which one understands.

Children are never fooled by empty praise and condescension. Ego identity gains real strength only from consistent feedback for real accomplishment that has meaning in the culture. Children who feel they are being deprived of forms of expression that allow them to grow will resist with astonishing strength. There is no feeling of being alive without a sense of identity.

Minority groups may be privileged to enjoy a more sensual early childhood (Erikson, 1950), but their crisis comes when their parents and teachers lose trust in themselves and create violent discontinuities (Rodriquez, 1982), or where children themselves learn to disavow their sensual and overprotective mothers as a barrier to the assimilation into the American culture which requires an American personality. The danger at this stage is identity (ethnic, sexual, etc.). Delinquency and psychotic incidents may occur. It sometimes results in running away, leaving school or job, staying out all night, or withdrawing into bizarre moods and/or drugs. Youth's greatest need and often only salvation is the professional's refusal to stereotype, pass social judgments, and diagnose in a pat fashion. These psychotic or criminal incidents in adolescence do not have the same fatal significance as at later stages. The expectation for failure very often brings just that result and becomes the wish-fulfilling fantasy.

## 6) *Intimacy and Distantiation vs. Self-Absorption*

When childhood comes to an end, the individual turns to work and/or study for a career, sociability with the opposite sex and, in time, marriage, and a family. Real intimacy with the opposite sex requires a reasonable sense of identity. When a youth does not accomplish such intimate relations with others and with his own inner resources in late adolescence or early adulthood, he may either isolate himself or at best find some highly stereotyped and formal interpersonal relations. The relationship will be lacking in spontaneity, warmth, and meaningful exchange.

The counterpart of intimacy is distantiation: the readiness to repudiate, to isolate, and if necessary to destroy those forces and people who seem dangerous.

## 7) *Generativity vs. Stagnation*

Generativity is primarily the interest in establishing and guiding the next generation. It deals with parenthood. This is seen as a stage in the growth of the healthy personality and, if it fails, regression from generativity may lead to an obsessive need for pseudointimacy, sometimes with a pervading sense of stagnation and interpersonal impoverishment. Individuals, then, often begin to indulge themselves as if they were their one and only child.

## 8) *Integrity vs. Despair and Disgust*

Integrity implies the acceptance of one's own and only life cycle, and of the people who have become significant to it. It thus means a new and different love of one's parents, free of the wish that they would be different, and it implies an acceptance that one's own life is one's own responsibility. The possessor of integrity is ready to defend the dignity of his own lifestyle against all physical and economic threats.

The loss of ego integration is signified by despair and an often unconscious fear of death. Such despair is often hidden behind a show of disgust or a chronic displeasure with particular institutions and people, all of which only signifies the individual's contempt of himself.

Erikson (1950) has emphasized that to develop a child with a healthy personality, a parent must be a "genuine" person living in a "genuine" milieu.

### D. O. HEBB: THE CONCEPTUAL NERVOUS SYSTEM

Hebb's theories have relevance for the learning-disabled child because of his suggestion that motivation is a physiological phenomenon. He emphasizes the need for different degrees of stimulation to activate the child's processing system.

Hebb's classic book, *Organization of Behavior* (1949), presents a theory based on the physiology of the nervous system correlating behavior and neural function. His concern is with the problem of thought as a process not fully controlled by environmental stimulation, yet cooperating closely with that stimulation. He postulates a central neural mechanism to provide for the transmission of sensory excitement to the motor areas through a "phase sequence" where stimulation leads to the development of a "cell assembly."

> . . . The assembly is thought of as a system inherently involving some equipotentiality, in the presence of alternate pathways, each having the same functions so that brain damage might remove some pathways without preventing the system from functioning particularly if the system has been long established. (Hebb, 1949, p. 74)

Hebb states that the human brain is built to be active and that activity motivates behavior. The activation or stimulation is a motivational process in itself. Behavioral problems tend to be the result of inactivity in the system. In some of the studies done by Hebb, where subjects were paid to be perceptually isolated, there was evidence of disorganized thought process and impaired problem solving. The lack of perceptual stimulation in these subjects became synonymous with a lack of arousal in a general drive state. The concept of drive is seen as anatomical and physiological.

Hebb has developed a concept of motivation as "the energizing of behavior." He describes the central nervous system as a very active one that becomes aroused by outer aspects (extrinsic drives) and inner aspects (intrinsic drives). Hebb sees any organized process in the brain as a motivated process. Motivation, according to him, is the energizing of behavior, where one particular set of responses is dominant over others. He makes a clear distinction between the cue and the arousal function. The cue can be the sensory stimuli and the arousal function the activation of the central nervous system to respond. For example, a person is lying in bed at night, and suddenly he smells smoke; the smoke is the cue. The arousal function activates the system to do something about it, get up, survey the situation, and call the fire department.

Hebb postulates another important concept which highlights the importance of the levels of drive intensity. At low levels, the increase of drive intensity is rewarding. In other words, if the stimulation is minimal, increasing it by using more positive cues would be more likely to energize the system. Conversely, if the stimulation is at a high level, it would have to be decreased in order for it to energize the system. A proper balance of stimulation, not too much or too little, enables the central nervous system to be activated.

Hebb also believes that where there are problems the central nervous system has the ability to reorganize so that response behavior can be more appropriate and properly organized. This reorganization can permit the entire system to function at a higher level.

## JEAN PIAGET AND HIS COGNITIVE THEORIES

Piaget (1929) dedicated himself to understanding the ways of human knowledge and to understanding intelligence as part of the process of biological adaptation. He concentrated on two main ideas: the growth of scientific knowledge and the intellectual development of the child. His task was to understand not only how ideas are attained, but how the intellect grows as a whole.

Piaget was not interested in psychometrics, but rather was intrigued by the processes whereby the child achieves correct answers. Psychiatric examining procedures were used to develop Piaget's *"méthode clinique"* by which much of Piaget's data have been collected. This method of intensive interrogation was common enough among psychiatrists, but even today it is likely to shock the American experimental psychologist trained in the canons of objectivity and standardization.

Another point of interest and concern was the employment of his own children as experimental subjects. This had particular significance because Watsonian behaviorism was, at that time, the most popular approach to understanding children's learning and growth. The behaviorist used a stimulus-response methodology as compared to Piaget's global field observational technique.

The range of Jean Piaget's writing is vast and includes the developmental aspects of language, perception, moral standards, motor behavior, intelligence, and cognition. Piaget's five important books of the 1920s and 1930s published in French caused a great flurry of interest in his work. These volumes—*Language and Thought of the Child* (1926), *Judgment and Reasoning of the Child* (1928), *The Child's Conception of the World* (1929), *The Child's Conception of Physical Causality* (1930), and *The Moral Judgment of the Child* (1932)—remain the cornerstones of his work.

In all of Piaget's works there are unifying trends and concerns. Apart from his zoological studies and a few mathematical papers on logic, his central preoccupation was with epistemology, the fundamental approach to how we come to know our world. This problem had been approached by Piaget via scientific observation and experimentation, although of an unconventional kind (Tuddenham, 1973). In the 1920s he took up the study of the child as an approach to fundamental epistemological questions and continued throughout his life to use infants, children, and adolescents as his subjects. The emphasis was always developmental. Piaget's epistemology is at once empirical and developmental in its orientation. Piaget observed and recorded, from earliest infancy to adolescence, how the child acquires strategies for coping with the real world.

In the early years, Piaget began the compilation of the forms of verbal expression characteristic of age levels from three to ten years. This led to the formulation that children's explanations of phenomena pass through stages from early animalistic, through magical and artificialist forms, to rational thought. At each level the child constructs a systematic cosmology according to the modes of reasoning available to him. In those early years, Piaget was subject to much criticism because of the nature of his method, which was to make observations of his own children, using verbalization to elicit responses. Piaget eventually shifted from verbal encounters to observation and experiment. This permitted him to study infants as well as older children.

Jean Piaget has probably made the most significant impact on the educational scene in the past decade. Central to Piaget's position is the concept of the organism passing through cognitive stages derived from motor action. The child is continually adding to his cognitive repertoire through the process of assimilation and accommodation. Piaget distinguishes four major stages in the development of intelligence: 1) the sensori-motor period, before the appearance of language, from birth to about two years; 2) the pre-operational period, from about two to seven years; 3) a period of concrete operations, from about seven to 12 years; and 4) the period of formal operations, about 12 years of age.

The sensori-motor stage carries the child from inborn reflexes to acquired behavior patterns. It leads the child from a body-centered world to an object-centered one. During this period of the development of object constancy, the various sensory spaces of vision, touch, and hearing are coordinated into a single space, and objects evolve from their separate sensory properties into things with multiple properties, permanence, and spatial relationships.

The pre-operational stage covers the important period when language is acquired. This permits the child to deal symbolically with the world, replacing direct motor action though his problem solving still tends to be "action ridden." The child himself is still the focus of his own world, and space and time are centered around him. Time is only "before now," "now," and "not yet," and space moves as the child moves. When he is taken for an evening walk, he thinks the moon follows *him*. Children, during this stage, gradually learn to conceive of a time scale and a spatial world which exist independently of them. During this stage, when dealing with objects, quantities, and words, the child pays attention to just one attribute while neglecting all others. He concludes, for example, that there is more water in a glass than in a beaker although he has seen the water poured from one vessel to the other. This is because in the beaker the column of water is taller, and the child neglects to pay attention to the other attribute, the reduction in diameter.

The stage of concrete operations reveals a child less dependent upon his own perceptions and motor actions. He begins to show capacity for reasoning, but on a concrete level. Among the child's logical acquisitions at this stage are classifying, ordering in a series, and numbering. Asked to put a handful of sticks in order by length, children no longer need to make all the pair comparisons but can pick out the longest, then the next longest, and so on. According to Piaget, the child has reached the ability to "conserve." At about 11 or 12 years of age, the child can handle abstract relationships while dealing with symbols instead of things, and can attend to the form of an argument while ignoring its content.

A principle central to Piaget's theories is that intellectual operations acquired by interaction between organism and environment develop in a lawful sequence. Piaget's efforts were to elucidate the sequence, not to establish age norms.

The innate equipment consists of reflexes present at birth. A few reflexes, such as yawning or sneezing, are relatively fixed and unmodifiable by experience, though some, like the Babinski, change with maturation. The majority of reflexes are modified as a result of experience, and these constitute the basic behavioral units from which more complex forms of behavior emerge (Tuddenham, 1973). According to Piaget, behavior is simultaneously determined by the inborn structure, past activations, experience, and the present situation to which the organism responds. When a reflex responds to such external stimuli, the total sensory, perceptual, and motor activities are incorporated into an existing schema, and this in turn modifies the particular schema involved. In other words, the organism experiences and reacts to the environmental stimulation always in terms of an existing organization. All experiences are molded into the reality conditions. This process Piaget called *assimilation and accommodation.* The taking in is called *assimilation. Accommodation* is described as the process by which a schema changes so as to adapt better to the assimilated reality.

Piaget's work on perception concerns itself with discovering the laws of perceptual development and the difference between perceptual and cognitive functions. To this end there have been 40 studies, chiefly on optical illusions, in which the traditional experimental approach was used. Piaget finds a general tendency, though by no means a linear one, for perceptual judgments to grow more accurate with age. He considers perceptual development as continuous and does not consider that the developmental stages, which are so important to his cognitive theory, exist in the perceptual domain. He has continually emphasized that the perceptual and cognitive domains follow different paths (Tuddenham, 1973).

Piaget has offered data to show that the age at which a particular stage is reached differs for different content. For example, with his general principle of conservation (i.e., invariance under transformation) of a plastic object such as a lump of clay, the child acquires it first with respect to mass, a year or so later with respect to weight, and a few years after that with respect to volume. He also noted that the age at which children reach these stages is different in different cultures. For example, the children in Montreal are years ahead in reaching each stage as compared to the children in Martinique. He insists, however, that the sequence remains the same (Laurendeau & Pinard, 1963).

One of the hallmarks of Piaget's work was his persistence and skill in bringing out the nonverbal aspects of thinking. Using his own three babies as sources, he studied the "logic of action" and the preverbal baby's slow construction (in stages) of fundamental categories for understanding the world: object, space, time, and causality. With older children, Piaget concentrated much of his attention on their long struggle, rarely verbalized in everyday life, to grasp the ways in which objects endure: the baby's emerging understanding that objects have a permanence (out of sight is not out of mind); the child's expanding grasp of the subtle and unspoken ways in which matter remains under various transformations (e.g., a clay ball squashed into a pancake does not change its weight).

Piaget's cognitive theory starts from the central postulate that motor action is the source from which mental operations emerge. The action of the organism is central to the acquisition of the operations (i.e., ideas or strategies) which one acquires for coping with the world. This theory places great emphasis upon the active interplay of organism and environment. Piaget's biological orientation is seen in his belief that intelligence is only one aspect of biological adaptation. Intelligence is seen as the organizing activity which extends the biological organization (Tuddenham, 1973).

Piaget (1952) writes, "Life is a continuous creation of increasingly complex forms, and a progressive balancing of these forms with the environment" (p. 3). Wolff (1960) states that Piaget considered intellectual adaptation as the progressive differentiation and integration of inborn reflex mechanisms under the impact of experience. It is this differentiation of inborn reflex structures and their functions that gives rise to the mental operations by which man conceives of objects, space, time, and causality, and of the logical relationships which are the basis for rational thought. For the learning-disabled child steps must be taken to provide more opportunities to have experiences at each level of operation.

## L. S. VYGOTSKY AND HIS THEORIES OF DEVELOPMENT

Lev Semyonovitch Vygotsky (1978) stressed the social origins of language and thinking, insisting that the culture in which one lives becomes a part of each person's nature. Vygotsky urged the combining of experimental cognitive psychology and neurology and physiology. Because Vygotsky studied all phenomena as processes in motion and in change, his theories offer insights into learning processes. The task, as he saw it, was to reconstruct the origin and course of the development of behavior and consciousness by tracing qualitative changes in behavior. According to Vygotsky, man through these behavioral changes comes to make nature serve his ends, and finally he can become the master.

The sign systems (language, writing, numbers, tools, etc.) are created by society and change with the forms of society and levels of cultural development. Sign symbols become the mediators in human interaction. Thus, the mechanism of individual developmental change is rooted in society and culture. The mediation process is central as the individual actively modifies stimulus situations as part of the process of responding to them. The child's system of activity is determined at each specific stage both by the child's degree of organic development and by his degree of mastery of the tools available. Symbolic activity has a specific organizing function that penetrates the process of tool use and produces new forms of behavior. Cole, John-Steiner, Scribner, and Souberman (1978) writing on Vygotsky's theories state:

> The most significant moment in the course of intellectual development which gives birth to the purely human forms of practical and abstract intelligence occur when speech and practical activity converge. The child begins to master his environment through the mediation of speech. This, in turn, produces new relations with the environment and new organizations of behavior. The creation of these new human forms of behavior later produce the *intellect* and become the basis for *productive work* (the human form of the use of tools). (pp. 24-25)

Vygotsky's unique contribution was to place psychology in a historical and cultural framework characterizing the human being's place in nature. Psychological processes, ordinarily thought to be special mental functions, were treated for the first time as complex forms of activity, the structure of which is provided by the structure of the social milieu, which in turn has been shaped by the social history of one's culture.

At the time of Vygotsky's work (the 1920s and 1930s), there was much controversy in psychology in many parts of the world, and Vygotsky referred to this as a "crisis in psychology." He dismissed the then current prevailing ideas in psychology that described: 1) the contents of human consciousness and their relation to human stimulation, analyzing various states of consciousness into their constituent elements defined as simple sensations (Wundt); 2) the studies of conditioned responses, substituting stimulus-response bonds for sensation (Watson); and 3) the study of perceptual phenomena (Kohler), all of which Vygotsky felt did not explain the complexity of the human organism.

Vygotsky, seeking a comprehensive approach acceptable to natural and social scientists, developed the Experimental Genetic Method. He conceived experiments in which the investigator created processes that telescope the actual course of development of a given function. He initiated experiments that provided an opportunity for the subjects to engage in a variety of activities so that they could be observed by the researcher while not being too rigidly controlled. He would then introduce obstacles into the task in order to disrupt the problem-solving methods of the subject—for example, a task situation requiring cooperative activity of children who did not share a common language (foreign-speaking or deaf children). In another experiment, he would use alternative routes to problem solving—for example, using different materials in order to study the external aids used by children of different ages and under different conditions. In still another research experiment, he set tasks before the child that he knew exceeded the child's knowledge and ability so that he might discover rudimentary beginnings of new skills. In all, Vygotsky's interest was in the process used by the child, not the performance or product achieved.

He studied the linkage between tool use and speech affecting several psychological functions, such as perception, sensory motor operations, and attention. He considered each of these to be part of a dynamic system of behavior. The connections and relations among functions constitute systems that change as radically in the course of a child's development as do the individual functions themselves.

According to Vygotsky, children describe pictures differently depending on their developmental stage. A two-year-old limits the description to separate objects within the picture. Older children describe actions and complex relationships. This suggests that the child's perceptual processes are initially fused and only later become differentiated.

Attention should be given major importance in the psychological structure underlying the use of tools. The ability or inability to direct and sustain one's attention is a determinant of success or failure on any task. The child's field of attention embraces a whole series of potential perceptual fields that form successive structures over time. Combining past and present visual fields (such as the tool and goal) in one field of attention leads to a basic reconstruction of another vital function, memory. The child's memory not only makes fragments of the past more available, but also results in a new method of uniting elements of past experience with the present. Created, with the help of speech, the field for action extends forwards and backwards. It creates the conditions for the development of a single system that includes effective elements of the past, present, and future. This emerging psychological system in the child now encompasses two new functions: intentions and symbolic representation of purposeful action. This change in the structure of the child's behavior is related to basic alterations in the child's needs and motivations. Thus the child's emotional thrust is shifted from a preoccupation with the outcome to the nature of the solution.

Unlike Piaget, Vygotsky was convinced that one could change the course of cognitive development through training. He suggested that rather than scoring intelligence tests in their standardized way, a better estimate of the individual's ability could be made after training was offered to enhance the score. He believed in the ability to change the intelligence quotient through teaching.

Vygotsky (1962) emphasized the relationship between education and development. He criticized the Piaget position that development and instruction are not related and that development takes place in age-related stages on which education has little if any influence. Piaget (1969) maintained that experiential factors can only become effective in the realm of development to the extent that they build on the child's previously developed structures of thought, as through the activation of a reasoning process prior to, but logically related to the one to be developed. Koffka (1966) has attempted to reconcile the two theories by stating that all development has two aspects, maturation and learning, and they are interdependent. He demonstrated that maturation of an organ is contingent on its functioning which improves through learning and practice.

## PIAGET'S DISCUSSION OF VYGOTSKY'S CRITICISMS

Working at approximately the same time as Piaget, Vygotsky (1962) outlined a dialectical-materialist (Marxist) theory of cognitive development. In many respects, it paralleled the work of Piaget and anticipated the more recent work of American social scientists. Vygotsky (1962) questioned some of the theoretical positions of Piaget, while agreeing with others. Piaget regretted very much that he did not become familiar with any of this criticism until after the death of Vygotsky in 1934. Piaget said that some of the criticism offered by Vygotsky was correct, and he himself came to understand it in his later formulations. Nevertheless, Piaget felt that Vygotsky's work emphasized too broadly the socialization and training process as being the most important factors in the development of cognition. Piaget (1962) wrote:

> It is not without sadness that an author discovers, twenty-five years later after its publication, the work of a colleague who has died in the meantime, when that work contains so many points of immediate interest to him which should have been discussed personally and in detail. . . . I have, however, found a solution both simple and instructive (at least for me), namely, to try and see whether or not Vygotsky's criticisms seem justified in the light of my later work. The answer is both yes and no: on certain points I find myself more in agreement with Vygotsky than I would have in 1934, while on other points I now have better arguments for answering him. When Vygotsky concluded from his reflections of my earliest books that the essential task of child psychology was to study the formation of scientific concepts in following step by step the process unfolding under our eyes, he had no inkling that that was my exact program. It is in what Vygotsky describes as the relationship of learning and develop-ment that he disagrees with me, though actually he differs with me only partly, and not in the sense he imagines but rather in the opposite sense. In the first place, he reproached me for view-ing school learning as not essentially related to the child's spon-taneous development. Yet it should be clear that to my mind it is not the child that should be blamed for the conflicts, but the school, unaware as it is of the use it could make of the child's spontaneous development, which it should reinforce by adequate methods instead of inhibiting it as it often does. In the second place—and this is Vygotsky's main error in his interpretation of my work—he believes that, according to my theory, adult thought, after various compromises, gradually supplants child thought, through some sort of mechanical abolition of the latter. Actually today I am more often blamed for interpreting spon-taneous development as tending toward the logico-mathematical structures of the adult as its predetermined ideal. (p. 1)

Vygotsky believed that new concepts are acquired through didactic intervention. Piaget disagreed. According to Piaget (1962), they are acquired in a so-called active school which endeavors to create situ-ations that, while not spontaneous in themselves, evoke spontaneous elaboration on the part of the child. If the child is motivated and if the problem is presented in such a way that it corresponds to the structures the child has already formed, the child learns new concepts.

## ALEXANDER R. LURIA: CEREBRAL ORGANIZATION OF MAN'S CONSCIOUS ACTION

Vygotsky's death in Russia in 1934 at the age of 37 left a large group of young scientists working in psychology, defectology, and mental abnormality. Alexander Luria was one such student who continued to carry on Vygotsky's research. Luria's study of brain processes led him to investigate problems of cognitive dysfunction. Because of this, he contributed much to the understanding of learning-disabled children.

Luria, like Vygotsky, grew up in a period of great turmoil in the Soviet Union. He entered the University when higher education was in the process of reconceptualization by the Soviet authority. Luria was strongly impressed by two contradictory schools of thought. First, he felt the need for objective methods of study but, at the same time, much of the objective psychological research he encountered seemed arid, devoid of the complex, emotion-ridden, highly organized behaviors that made people exciting objects of analysis. Having read the works of Freud and Jung, he tried to bridge some of the psychoanalytic theories with the goals of experimental science. This line of research served as the basis for part of his first book, *The Nature of Human Conflict* (1932).

The central idea of the book was that human emotions cannot be simulated for laboratory experiments. Artificial events can only evoke excitation, not relate to real-life behavior. He suggested that emotions ought not to be studied directly as psychological phenomena but rather via their effect on ongoing voluntarily controlled behavior. Luria then developed a laboratory technique called "the combined motor method." For example, a simple voluntary response such as squeezing the rubber bulb was required following the signal from the experimenter. When the response to a simple command, "squeeze," became automatic to the subject, verbal stimuli of greater interest were introduced, and the subject was required to free associate while continuing to respond to each stimulus by squeezing the bulb. He combined the affective domain with almost a classical conditioning of squeezing the bulb.

While interested in the latency and the content of the verbal response, Luria's special purpose was to determine the way in which the affect aroused by the verbal stimulus disrupted the flow of the response. With this technique in hand, he went on to develop laboratory methods of real-life conflict situations. For example, when the educational authorities of Moscow University decided to purge the student body of those who had gotten by with too little academic work or whose family background disqualified them, Luria and his colleagues were there to conduct their research. Taking people out of the line of those awaiting interrogation, they plied them with verbal stimuli whose emotion-inducing actions they could be certain of, such as examining, expelling, purging—all very heavy emotional inputs. Later this same technique was used with criminals awaiting interrogation. These studies brilliantly illustrate the kind of psychology that was to be one of Luria's unique contributions.

Part three of *The Nature of Human Conflict* (1932) is a formulation of the issues that were to occupy Luria throughout the remainder of his career: the role of speech in the development and organization of mental processes. In retrospect, one can see that Luria here was introducing the reader to the basic concepts introduced by Vygotsky, his mentor and colleague. He introduced such ideas as the brain correlates of behavior and the development of intellect.

In the early 1930s, the cultural and historical context of psychological activity was the object of Luria's research in two expeditions to Central Asia, where traditional pastoral culture was being transformed by massive collectivization, literacy campaigns, and formal schooling. Luria's report of a qualitative shift in psychological functioning as a result of the cultural change that peasants were undergoing was consistent with Vygotsky's theory.

Luria (1976) attempted to create a "romantic science," in which general laws derived from laboratory research would have to confront the "living facts" that they were supposed to explain. Luria created a system, part clinical and part experimental, designed to produce data adequate to the phenomena being analyzed. He stated that the scientific observation is to see and understand the way a thing or event relates to other things and events. To Luria it was not enough to probe an event if it was isolated from other experiences. The model system he created attempted to teach children thinking skills and strategies somewhat separate from the usual three R's curricula. The results of this research showed that children provided evidence for a new pedagogy which stressed interactive learning in which the principal element was guided social interaction.

The years immediately following Vygotsky's death in 1934 were especially difficult for his students. As a result of furor over the work in Central Asia, partly because of strong reaction against psychological testing, Luria's work veered in a number of unexpected directions. For example, he began to work out of the Medico-Genetic Institute and was carrying out pioneering studies with identical and fraternal twins in an effort to disentangle natural and culturally shaped psychological processes as they interact over the course of human ontogeny. This line of work ran into political problems because of the prevailing emphasis on environmental influence. Luria then decided to complete his medical training, and upon completion of medical school he worked in a neurological clinic. These vicissitudes in his training prepared Luria to make maximum use of the tragic opportunities for brain research that arose when Germany attacked the Soviet Union in 1941. For the next years he worked in surgical wards, where he studied diagnosis and restoration of disruptive brain functions arising from head wounds. This experience served as the foundation upon which his reputation as a neurologist was based. *The Man With a Shattered World* (1972) is the story of one such wounded soldier who had his brain shattered, and it traces the struggle to try to revitalize the functions that were no longer available.

In the late 1940s, events again intervened and Luria turned from neuropsychology to the study of developmental abnormalities associated with mental retardation. This period coincided with the Soviet Union's emphasis on medical and social sciences, and the use of Pavlovian neuropsychological concepts was demanded of all researchers. Luria's writing reflected the influence of these requirements. Fortunately, Pavlov's speculations about the influence of language on the structure of reflex processes in human beings were similar to Vygotsky's ideas about the mediated process and the nature of higher psychological processes. Luria found enough similarity to permit him to pick up a line of research that had lain dormant for many years.

In the late 1950s, the times again permitting, Luria returned to the area of neuropsychology, which remained his major concern until the time of his death. Throughout his long and difficult career, Luria devoted enormous energy to psychology as an international human enterprise.

Luria has contributed widely to the field of neuropsychology and psychology. One of his major contributions has been his view of brain processes. Luria saw the functioning of the brain as a global, activated process in constant flow and activity even though there were isolated, localized functions. The brain is seen as a "dynamic localization of local functions" (Luria, 1973, p. 116), a working constellation of local functions interwoven and interchanged so that anything that affects one local area has an effect on the whole brain. Luria described the brain as a dynamic orchestration where one can listen and follow the notes of one instrument, but that instrument can only be understood as it relates to the entire musical orchestration.

Luria (1973) theorized that there are three basic blocks to the working brain. The first and developmentally earliest block includes the upper brain stem, the reticular formation, and the oldest part of the limbic cortex and hippocampus. He called it the *block of energy and tone*. This block is responsible for the stable tone of the cortex and for the state of vigilance. It includes a considerable number of neurons which react to every change of stimuli and are sometimes called "attention units." Patients with lesions in this area manifest marked disturbances in stable wakefulness, instability of memory trace, and selective organization of thinking similar to what is observed in dreaming states. These lesions do not result in any basic disturbances of the structure of concepts nor in a primary loss of simple programs which control conscious action. In these cases, a slight reinforcement increasing the lowered cortical tone may easily lead to a compensation of the defects and to a recovery of the deranged control of behavior.

The second block of the brain includes the posterior parts of the hemispheres with the occipital, parietal, and temporal regions as well as their underlying structures. It can be defined as a block of the *input, recoding, and storage of information* received from the external and proprioceptive world. The systems of this block are modality specific. For example, the occipital lobe is a central device for visual analysis and never takes part in the decoding of acoustic signals.

Patients with lesions of the posterior part of the brain may lose several important behavioral operations, but these lesions *never result* in a general deterioration of their conscious behavior. These patients retain their plans and strategies. They are fully aware of their defects and very actively try to overcome them. Luria concluded that the second basic block of the brain is in no way responsible for the regulation and control of man's conscious behavior.

The third block of the brain includes the *frontal lobes,* and it is the last acquisition in the evolutionary process. It occupies nearly one third of the brain stem, being densely supplied with ascending and descending fibers. Their medio-basal parts may be regarded as an important cortical structure superimposed on the systems of the upper brain stem. The structure of this block becomes mature only during the period which is of decisive significance for the acquisition of the first forms of conscious control of behavior: "There are many reasons to suppose that this block of the brain plays an important role in the realization of the plans and programs of human actions and in the regulation and the control of human behavior" (Luria, 1973, p. 118).

As a rule, patients with *severe* lesions of the prefrontal areas do not manifest any stable alterations of memory and orientation in the immediate environment (these are more typical of patients with lesions in the medial parts of the hemisphere). They do not suffer any defects in perception, movement, speech, or even logical operations. At first glance one would suspect they preserve all basic functions, but that is not so. Observation shows the severity of the disturbance in the regulation and control of the conscious behavior of these patients. They lack strategies and are unable to create plans or follow programs. They substitute primitive, impulsive responses to immediate stimuli and find it difficult to adjust to new situations. Luria (1973) gives the example of "a woman with a massive bilateral tumor of the frontal lobe who at an early stage of her disease was seen to stir burning coal with a broom and to cook some of the bristles instead of noodles" (p. 124). Another example is of "a soldier with a massive bilateral gunshot wound of the frontal lobes who started to plane a plank but could not stop and automatically continued this work until almost half of the bench itself proved to be planed down" (Luria, 1973, p. 119). It is clear that the purposeful forms of conscious behavior were replaced here by uncontrolled responses to immediate impressions or by automatic, inert stereotypes.

Luria also suggested the likelihood that the frontal lobes play an important role in the regulation of vigilance required for the realization of complicated intellectual actions. This was corroborated by a series of experiments by Walter (1966) in England and Livanov (1966) in the USSR. Walter's studies showed that any expectations of a signal evoke a special kind of slow potential which appears in the subject's frontal lobes and subsequently spreads to the posterior parts of the cortex. Walter (1966) called them *expectancy waves*, and he observed their intensification when the subject's activity increased and their disappearance when the instruction ended. Livanov (1966), in Moscow, confirmed the same observations. Using a 50-channel amplifier when he gave the subject a difficult intellectual task, he saw a significant number of synchronously excited points appeared in the subject's frontal lobes. These disappeared when the problem was solved. Luria and Homskaya (1966) showed that the frontal lobes played a significant part in the regulation of the active states started by a verbal instruction.

Thus, Luria agreed with Hebb's assumption that the human central nervous system is really a conceptual nervous system and that its basic task consists of elaborating some inner codes which result in the execution of certain plans and programs, and in the regulation and control of man's own behavior. This makes the human brain, according to Luria (1973), an "organ of freedom" (p. 126).

For the purposes of this book, it is important to return to Luria's earlier work, *The Role of Speech in the Regulation of Normal and Abnormal Behavior* (1961). This makes clear that the highest form of self-regulatory behavior does not lie in the depths of the organism but instead in the complex interaction of a child's relations with his social environment and his acquisition of language. Luria (1973) states that the role of speech is a beginning step toward self-regulatory behavior.

Luria reaffirms Vygotsky's notions of child development. A newborn child begins its life with a series of innate self-regulatory systems of a very elementary type—breathing and sucking, primitive orienting reflexes. The newborn starts living in immediate social contact with adults. The mothering person constantly speaks to the child. She shows an object, points to it, names it, and the child may turn his eyes to the object. She then may ask the child to point to the named object, or she might say, "Give the ———— to me." The child's conscious action is divided between the mother and itself. Subsequently, the child begins to use his own language, singling out the object and then naming it. The function formerly divided between mother and child becomes now a new form of an inner self-regulated psychological process. This new behavior on the part of the child is social in origin, but becomes verbally mediated and self controlled by the child. This is only the beginning of a long process in higher psychological functions. At the beginning stage, the verbal command can start an action but is unable to overcome the immediate influences of the inertia of already established stereotypes.

In the course of many experimental programs with children (20 months to four years) giving verbal instructions requiring a motor response, it became clear that for success the child's motor reactions needed to evoke a feedback signal with information concerning the result of the task. For example, if Luria instructed the child to "press the bulb in order to put out the light" instead of what he originally asked ("When you see a red light, press the bulb"), the child was able to complete the task successfully. Thus, at this early stage of development, a verbal program could be realized only when reinforced by a feedback signal of the action fulfilled. In this case, "press the bulb" produced lights out and the child needed to see the results of his action.

The next question Luria addressed was: Can the feedback signal be replaced by the child's own verbal commands as a means of control? Negative results were obtained with two-year-olds, but positive results were obtained when the children reached three years two months of age. The child then, to his own command "Go-go," began to produce organized motor pressures and to block uncontrolled movements. This was the first manifestation that overt speech could act as a regulator of human behavior. If the experiments were made more complicated, negative results were obtained. Therefore, a stage can be described when the immediate discharging role of the child's own verbal command dominates over the semantic role of his speech. Further development is needed to make this semantic side of the child's speech a predominant one. The ultimate stage is reached only at about four years of age when children begin to form some inner programs of complex actions and when their own overt speech becomes a less decisive factor. The semantic programs based on children's inner speech begin to acquire their controlling functions, and the child becomes able to fulfill the programs of simple choice reactions even without his own overt verbal reinforcement. This stage is of great significance as it is the first step toward the consolidation of the inner controlling mechanisms of the child's conscious action.

Luria took the language formulation one more step. He attempted to provide a precise psychophysical method—a neurodynamic approach to the analysis of development of verbal regulation of behavior. The verbal regulatory mechanism for human behavior is seen as the force behind man's conscious actions. Luria stated (1960):

> . . . development as a whole is a kind of interiorization of social conduct, creating new levels of behavior in man. . . . The first stage is when the child's verbal activity cannot yet play a decisive role in the organization of his own behavior. The second step is when the child's verbal activity begins to play a regulating influence on his behavior, but is not yet complete. At this second stage, the semantic side of speech does not yet have a decisive influence . . . at this third stage, it is not obligatory for the child to apply externally vocalized speech, because at the moment when semantic control is developed, the child can use his internal subvocal speech. As a result of this interiorized process, the child can obey instructions without speaking loudly and without using the reinforcement of his own externally heard speech. (p. 392)

Luria points out that speech has different roles—a nominative role, a generalizing or semantic role, a communicatory role and a regulating role. The regulating role is the least known but, according to Luria, is very important in exploring the problem of mutual relationships of what he calls the "two signalling systems."

Luria's theory that the verbal regulatory mechanism is central to human behavior has generated the idea that the communication system plays a vital role in the behavior and treatment of the learning-disabled child.

## HEINZ WERNER: THE ORGANISMIC DEVELOPMENTAL FRAMEWORK

The vast body of research of Heinz Werner encompasses all areas of normal and deviant development, including studies of language, thought, perception, adaptation, and emotion. Much of his work has contributed to and fostered research in learning disability, perception, and cognition. He was influenced by Piaget, Freud, and Lewin, and in turn tried to integrate many of the important concepts of his time.

His Orthogenetic theory states the following progression of growth:

> . . . organisms are naturally directed towards a series of trans-formations . . . reflecting a tendency to move from a relative globality and undifferentiatedness towards states of increasing differentiation and hierarchical integration. (Werner & Kaplan, 1963, p. 7)

The basic assumptions underlying this theory are: 1) that any organ or activity is dependent upon the context, field, or whole of which it is a part; 2) that the various organs or activities of an organism function in the realization of ends immanent in the activity of the organism (its directedness); 3) that development is a constitutive mo-ment of organismic functioning stressing the orthogenetic principle above; and 4) that such developmental changes entail both continuity and discontinuity, that is to say that they are continuous in terms of an increase in differentiation and hierarchical integration and discon-tinuous in terms of the specific concrete forms and operations.

Werner (1957) states:

> . . . according to the above principle a state involving a relative lack of differentiation between subject and object is develop-mentally prior to one in which there is a polarity of subject and object. . . . This increasing subject object differentiation in-volves a corollary that the organism becomes increasingly less dominated by the immediate concrete situation; the person is less stimulus-bound and less impelled by his own affective status. A consequence of this freedom is the clearer understanding of goals, the possibility of employing substitutive means and alter-native ends. There is hence a greater capacity for delay and planned action. (p. 127)

According to Werner, this enables the person to manipulate the environment rather than passively respond to it. This freedom from the domination of the immediate situation permits a more accurate assessment of others and less tendency to interpret the world solely in terms of one's own needs. The Marble Board Test (Strauss &

Lehtinen, 1947) developed by Werner is an invaluable tool to help detect brain-injured subjects and their modes of response. Their performance can reveal a rigidity of behavior, an inability to respond to the needs of others, and concrete, stimulus-bound responses, all of which can confirm a breakdown in the organismic developmental structure.

Werner (1957) provides us with the framework within which to understand the full impact of causative factors, the development of deviant growth and learning patterns, and the rationale behind differential diagnosis and different treatment methodologies.

Werner (1957) tells us that as children mature they move from a state of global perception and reaction to increasing differentiation and hierarchical organization. Infants initially perceive their world in a global fashion. As children learn to differentiate increasingly between themselves and other objects and people, they become less dominated by the surrounding stimulus field and are more able to define themselves. They develop concepts about themselves and their world, and in this way achieve freedom to organize and control behavior in themselves and the world about them. They begin to experience the power they have over their environment. Werner discusses the "holistic approach," one in which there is a reciprocal relationship between the organism and its environment. Werner uses the term "directiveness assumption" to mean the tendency of organisms to conserve their integrity and develop toward a mature state. Each organism forms his "Umvelt," allowing the person to learn to cope with his own environment. This requires a congruity, a balance between the means and the ends, permitting the person to solve his own life problems. It implies that in order to study a child one must look at the child in relationship to his total environment, and not at just one element at a time. Maturation is seen as a continuous and discontinous flow toward growth, just like the flow of a river: There may be barriers—sticks, stones, logs—which may hold back the flow for a while (discontinuity), but eventually the river continues its natural way (continuity). As maturation proceeds, the child moves from undifferentiated to differentiated; through continuous-discontinuous-continuous growth; through periods of hierarchical integration in an upward maturational spiral. The continuous quality is the increasing maturation, and the discontinuous might be the specific normal functions and structures that impede the maturational striving upward.

Werner describes this in terms of developmental transformations "from reflexive reactions to sensory-motor action" (infants' response to stimulus) to "goal directiveness," during which period the infant acts upon signals or stimuli. In the first stage he is reaching toward, in the second he is acting upon. The third stage, according to Werner, is a more contemplative, reflective one. Last, he describes the maturational stage during which one begins to learn to manipulate one's environment and gains control over it.

An illustration of one of his many well-known experiments helps clarify the nature of Werner's thinking. He was interested in the development of the acquisition of meaning. He imbedded an artificial word in six verbal contexts to see when children between the ages of eight and 13 years could gain meaning from this artificial word. For example, Werner created the word "corplum" and began by placing it in a meaningful context:

1) A corplum may be used for support.
2) Corplums may be used to close off an open place.
3) A corplum may be long or short, thick or thin, strong or weak.
4) A wet corplum does not burn.
5) You can make a corplum smooth with sandpaper.
6) The painter uses a corplum to mix his paints.

The younger child needed more clues to solve the task. Werner concluded that it takes a synthesis of clues to acquire meaning. It requires the child to draw upon the knowledge already known, to transfer it, and integrate a new idea into a body of knowledge.

The organismic-developmental framework of Heinz Werner, though a unitary one, consists of the coordinationn and integration of two orientations, one organismic-holistic, the other developmental. Two general assumptions underly the nature of behavior. One is the *holistic* one which maintains that any local organ or activity is dependent upon the context, field, or whole of which it is a constitutive part, its properties and functional significance determined by the larger whole or context. The second general assumption is that of directiveness; the various organs or activities of an organism function in the realization of ends imminent in the activity of the organism as a whole. The nature of an organism's *Umvelt* is determined by the "ends" of the organism and by its species—specific and individual apparatus for engaging in transactions with its surroundings. It is also dependent on the physical geographic environment.

This organismic-holistic orientation is closely interwoven with a developmental orientation. It is assumed that organisms are naturally directed towards a series of transformations, reflecting the tendency to move from a state of relative globality and undifferentiatedness toward states of increasing differentiation and hierarchical integration. It is this tendency formulated by Werner (1957) as the *orthogenetic principle* which serves to characterize development as distinct from other types of change over time.

One finds that, with development, local activities become more and more interrelated and integrated; that is, become more and more under the control of goal-directed activities of the organism. Concurrently the nature of the organism-environment transactions undergoes marked changes.

At the postnatal human level, with the emergence of a basic directiveness towards knowing, man's hand and brain participate in the construction of tangible tools out of the properties of the environment and the construction of precepts and concepts which mediate between man and his physical milileu. It is primarily toward these objects that man's distinctive behavior is oriented. The symbol, the most significant of man's instrumentalities, is formed from this context.

## SUMMARY OF DEVELOPMENTAL THEORIES

All of the developmental theorists presented have contributed to the formulation of the Clinical Teaching Model.

Gesell has helped the professional to understand the embryology of behavior and the adaptation of the organism. He has suggested that training has little effect on development. Anna Freud provides us with a framework for understanding uneven development and its effect on learning. She enables us to understand the defenses children employ to protect themselves from failure or loss of self-esteem. Erikson relates the biological and social conflicts children experience growing up in our society. If these conflicts go unresolved, they will affect the learning process. Piaget offers a comprehensive study of intellectual development and categorizes the stages through which children pass in order to achieve intellectual competence. Vygotsky and Luria present knowledge of brain processes, and Luria in particular contributes information about the effect brain dysfunction may have on many aspects of learning and behavior. Hebb's theory of motivation gives us insight into the importance of the amount of stimulation needed to arouse the central nervous system and suggests that individuals need differing degrees of stimulation to respond. Werner, in a large body of research, has developed a comprehensive system which combines knowledge from physiology, psychology, and neurology, and applies the information to learning and growth.

All of these theorists have something important to contribute to our knowledge of the learning-disabled child. Each enables us to understand more fully what is normal within each child and to use these normal functioning areas to help compensate for the dysfunctional areas.

# CHAPTER 5

# Theoretical Considerations in Assessment: Ways to Observe Children

The Clinical Teaching Model accepts that children have differing constitutions, which are more or less sensitive to pain and stress. For the child who is more sensitive, the way the environment supports him may make the difference in his later cognitive as well as emotional development. Problems of many children tend to be difficult to trace because of this chaining reaction. The very nature of the developmentally changing organism and children's changing attitudes in their relationship with important mothering or nurturing persons make the tracing more difficult (Sapir & Nitzburg, 1973).

## ETIOLOGIES OF LEARNING DISABILITIES

Pasamanick and Knobloch (1964) describe "reproducible causality" (p. 108) as the chaining of such events as the mother's constitution, nutrition, and adaptability; prenatal factors in health care and nutrition; and the important postnatal, first-year experience. Poor nutrition or health care may result in damage to the fetus or newborn infant, generally in the central nervous system. This chaining tends to occur more frequently in the lower socioeconomic groups, producing children who are more susceptible to reproductive causality. Pasamanick and Knobloch also emphasize that males are more likely than females to have problems: More are conceived and aborted; more have difficulty during birth; and more are damaged and lost in the first year of life. Pasamanick has suggested that the higher percentage of reading problems in the male, as compared to the female, may well be the result of this susceptibility. He recognizes that life experiences and the social-cultural milieu are also factors to be considered in the proliferation of such problems.

Richardson (1966) has stressed the social factors which lead to lags in development. He cites a large body of research which relates childhood mortality, morbidity, and handicapping conditions to social-environmental factors. His review of research supports the thesis that social-environmental conditions can influence the growth and development of children both socially and biologically.

Cravioto (1966) emphasizes the essential importance of the quality of the nutrition to the psychobiological development of children. He gathered a large body of information which indicated the effects of malnutrition upon development. Children who have previously been malnourished seemed to be stunted in growth, to exhibit psychological derangement, and to be delayed in some aspects of their biochemical maturation. Cravioto and Robles (1965) sought to assess the psychological test performance of children who were severely malnourished during three different age periods: between birth and six months, between six months and 30 months, and after 30 months. Their results suggest that infants that suffered protein calorie malnutrition before the age of six months had persistently low performance scores during the experimental period. When the period of malnutrition occurred after six months of age, the initial deficit in intellectual potential completely disappeared, provided other factors did nt interfere. Cravioto, DeLicardie, and Birch (1966) later carried out a cross-sectional study of the total primary school of a rural Guatemalan village in which there was evidence of acute or prolonged malnutrition in preschool children. Their findings tend to confirm the circular effect of deprivation:

> The net result of nutritional deprivation and social impover-
> ishment is what in an ecological sense could be called a circular
> effect. A low level of adaptive capacity or ignorance or social
> custom results in malnutrition and produces a large number of
> people whose functioning is suboptimal and who are themselves
> more ready to be the victims of ignorance and less effective in
> social adaptation than would otherwise be the case. In turn, they
> may rear children under similar conditions and in a fashion that
> will produce a new generation of malnourished children. (Cra-
> vioto, 1966, p. 53)

Cravioto and Arrieta (1981) add another dimension to these findings as their research extends to include infant stimulation as well as mal-nutrition as a factor in mental development. They state that there has been a tendency to view the relationship between nutritional status and socioeconomic conditions circularly and to conclude that the ab-normal outcome in growth, development, and learning found in sur-vivors of early malnutrition can be attributed to social status. They emphasize that the finding of an association between early malnutri-tion and lags in mental development does not constitute evidence that insufficient intake of nutrients and calories is causally related to mental competence, or to learning and behavior. They state that, within this context, even the role of food and feeding should be considered as having at least three dimensions: 1) a physiological dimension, in which the unit of measurement is the nutrient; 2) the psychological dimension, where the unit of measurement is the food which provides stimuli such as texture, color, aroma, flavor, and temperature; and 3) the psychosocial dimension, in which the unit of measurement is mealtime, which aids in the formation of symbols through the value the family places on food as a reward or punishment. In addition, the mealtime provides opportunities for demonstration, clarification, and practice of the role and status of different individuals within the family and at the community level. Cravioto and Arrieta (1981) conclude that food deprivation in young children represents not only a shortage of the nutrients necessary for increase in body mass but also a deprivation of sensory stimuli and of social experiences. In their findings, the physical characteristics of the children's parents, family structure, economics of the family, sanitary conditions, mother's cleanliness, and literacy *did not* distinguish between families with severely malnourished children and those well nourished. In their research other factors, such as radio listening by the mother, the amount and type of stimulation available in the home, and the mother's behavior toward the child helped substantially to identify those families with and without potentially severely malnourished children long before the appearance of the disease.

Gardner (1971) took the theme of deprivation one step further in exploring the impact of deprivation on the cognitive-affective structures. He expands the concept of deprivation beyond the external, environmental, ecological variables that do not promote the individual's optimal development. He widens the definition of deprivation to include the absence of certain requirements for effective adaptation, and relates this to the organism's need to be in a state of "organismic equilibrium" (p. 484). Gardner describes the child's deprivation as just being born into a world that makes demands of a cognitive-affective nature. He makes a plea that we understand brain-damaged children as "battered heroes of evolution" (p. 124) and regard with awe their continuing attempts to adapt in the face of staggering difficulties.

Masland (1967) attempts to show the relationship between the problems of language and the underlying structures and brain mechanisms upon which language depends. He emphasizes the interrelationships of the entire mechanism and states:

> There are two ways of studying a mechanism. One is to put something into the input and study what comes out. . . . The other is to remove the cover and see what you can learn about the world which are [sic] inside. (p. 85)

Weil (1970) emphasizes that language develops out of the early communication system between the mother/caretaker and child. If this communication system falters for whatever reason, language development will also probably be affected.

Freeman (1967) gives a comprehensive picture of the emotional reactions of handicapped children. He demonstrates the causal relationships between physical factors and emotional development, and shows how any one factor can repeatedly influence the course of a deviant growth pattern through each developmental stage.

In the first few months, the handicapped child may show alterations that are puzzling and frightening to the parents. Rhythmicity of certain functions may not be so readily established and may interfere with smooth mother-child interaction. While the normal child may be developing a sense of "basic trust" that his needs will be met, the child with developmental deviations may sense the world as chaotic, painful, unsatisfying. This might contribute to later maladaptive behavior. Between the ages of three and six years, some handicapped children of this age become aware that they are being surpassed by a younger sibling, and they see that they are different, yet very few adults are prepared to discuss this with the children.

## ETIOLOGIES OF BRAIN DYSFUNCTIONS

Weil (1970) distinguishes between congenital and acquired brain dysfunctions. With respect to the congenital conditions, there are developmental lags as well as immaturities. Developmental lags reveal a slowness and initial deficiency in the maturation of certain centers, with consequent clinical lag in the development of the corresponding functions. These developmental lags may affect movement and speech, and later, reading and writing. In cerebral palsy, slowness with deficient motor function sometimes can be associated with spasticity or weakness of the muscles. In children with developmental aphasias or dysphasias, delays in language development are found. With such children, one of the important steps is the distinction between autism and aphasic disturbances. The autistic child is withdrawn, wants solitary play, rejects attempts at interaction, and tends to push a helping hand away or may go into a temper when help is offered. Children who are aphasic may be warm and reachable (if not secondarily traumatized), maintain eye contact, respond to suggestions, and try to make themselves understood. Frustrations, however, can lead to temper tantrums. Dysphasic children may not express the right word. Instead, they may utter identical combinations of sounds or a word for another object within the same general category (e.g., "shirt" for "pants").

Another developmental lag may be the alexias or dyslexias, as represented by those children who are not ready to learn to read if they have not been traumatized. This does not assume that all dyslexias are developmental lags; there may be many other causes. In many cases, these developmental lags may show improvement if secondary emotional problems are kept at a minimum.

Weil (1970) suggests that acquired brain dysfunctions can be prenatal, perinatal, or postnatal. Specific etiologies in children suspected of learning disability may be inflammatory, traumatic, and anoxemic in nature. Inflammatory infections, such as encephalitis or any other infectious disease, especially with high fever before the age of two, can lead to subsequent complications. Traumata imply birth injuries as well as later head injuries. Anoxemia is thought of here as the inability of the premature (birth weight below five pounds) infant's circulation to support an adequate oxygen supply to the brain.

The typical behavior of children with learning disabilities is hyperkinetic although there are those who show lethargy and hypokinesis. The typical hyperkinesis of these children has been called "an organic drivenness of brain stem origin" (Kahn & Cohen, 1943). The brain reacts to damage as a whole, and this total reaction consists of impairment of basic patterns of integration and synchronization as well as of the inhibitory function of the cortex (Weil, 1970). This often leads to less controlled behavior with primitive exaggerated impulses, making for "organic drivenness" and "catastrophic reactions" (Goldstein, 1942).

Weil (1970) states:

Many of these children exhibit not only a great degree of restlessness, but also a constant desire to contact the environment, to take, touch or destroy; to cling, nag or to be overaffectionate. Probably the hyperkinesis is supported by a need to re-experience—a need which may be due to such children's disturbance in perception (foreground, background disturbance) and their inability to integrate their experiences into meaningful concepts according to their age. Dysfunctions in the area of language of speech will further spur trends toward hyperactiveness. Dysnomias and language difficulties foster discharge in action (at an age when verbalization would normally take over) and this tendency toward action then interacts unfavorably with the child's general basic hyperkinetic drivenness. Often there is impulsiveness, lack of restraint and inhibitions, which sometimes may lead to a poor social behavior. In general, however, a child with minimal brain dysfunction, although irritable, demanding and unable to stand frustrations, may at the same time express a wish to do right. In line with the general restlessness and impulsiveness and the inability to integrate diverse stimuli, such a child is distractible, inattentive, and often has difficulty adjusting in a group and learning according to his capacities. The entire picture is usually overlaid by a diffuse anxiety, partly of organic "brain stem drivenness," partly exaggerated by the child's inability to comply with expectations and to adjust to, as well as live up to, his peers. (p. 91)

## PRINCIPLES OF ASSESSMENT

The position taken in the Clinical Teaching Model is that diagnosis should not be divorced from treatment and should become an essential part of clinical education and teaching. This is not to suggest that a working knowledge of standardized psychometric tests (intelligence, achievement, attitude, projective and personality, perceptual and cognitive language tests) is not essential. Rather it means that a working knowledge of the interpretations of the standardized test data *alone* may be inadequate to help a learning-disabled child (Sapir & Nitzburg, 1973). Vygotsky (1962) has said that a test of a child's ability rests with understanding what the child can do, observing where he has difficulty, teaching him when he needs help, and evaluating how much he has learned and how he has mastered the tasks. Put another way, one must understand and observe what process children use, their hierarchy of strengths and weaknesses, and what happens when you teach them. Teaching may then become the best diagnostic tool of all. In this way, one can look for the "islands of health" in the child. Using the child's strengths to help him compensate for his deficits is the basis of this position.

This approach does not categorize or label a child. It is an ongoing assessment, because, as the child matures, change takes place. The new observations lead to further refinement of the assessment strategies. This method assumes that developmental variations and environmental influences interact continuously, revealing their impact along different dimensions of growth. As children adapt to the challenges they encounter, competence emerges.

Professionals can increase their ability to help children through enhanced awareness of some important dimensions of learning.

## ASSESSING THE DIMENSIONS OF LEARNING
## AND GROWTH: OBSERVING CHILDREN

The dimensions of observation are as follows:

Physical/Motor
Temperament
Affect/Personality
Social Interaction
Perception
Cognition/Language
Academic Skills

These dimensions may be viewed as basic to the understanding of each child's potential as well as to his learning style. It should be understood that the dimensions isolated here for purposes of definition are in reality intertwined. It is the interplay among dimensions that most richly reveals the whole child. The illustrations offered are intended to highlight each dimension definition rather than to be all-inclusive.

### *Physical/Motor*

Children's physical makeup, their general level of body tone and coordination, articulatory mechanism, eye-tracking ability, and gross and small motor coordination play a vital role in the children's exploration of their environment and the development of their self-esteem.

For illustration, one can contrast a child with excellent physical coordination, clear articulation of sounds, quick reflex responses, and a sense of competence in this dimension with a child who is clumsy, has muffled, inarticulate speech, has difficulty making things with his hands, and has limited confidence in his motor ability.

*Temperament*

Using the nine temperamental characteristics as described by Thomas, Chess, and Birch (1967) as yardsticks in our observations of children, we can draw a clear picture of the child's innate temperamental qualities. The nine characteristics are activity level, rhythmicity, distractibility, approach-withdrawal, adaptability, attention span and persistence, intensity of reaction, threshold of responsiveness, and quality of need. These innate characteristics are apparent almost from birth and remain relatively constant over time. They affect all learning experiences. Especially significant for children with learning problems are their threshold of responsiveness (the intensity of stimuli necessary to evoke a response), attention span and persistence (length of time an activity will be pursued by the child), level of distractibility (the impact of extraneous stimuli), and tempo (slow or fast pace of the child).

For illustration, one can think of a hyperactive child, impulsive with poor attention, distractible and unable to focus on the task at hand as compared to children who are passive, slow paced, and who need much stimulation to engage them in an activity.

*Affect/Personality*

The child's self-concept and feelings of adequacy are key to this dimension. The nature of the child's responses to deeply felt life experiences and the way the child defends himself against failure are the key to the analysis of the personality of the child. Feelings of inadequacy may be expressed in many ways, such as hiding, clowning, denial, or aggression.

One child may express his sense of inadequacy through body language rather than verbalization and strike out aggressively against others. Another very verbal child may become negative, expressing distress through denial or withdrawal.

*Social Interaction*

The child's interactions with peers and adults profoundly influence learning and growth. The effectiveness of the verbal and nonverbal communication system, the ability to adapt to varying social experiences, and the ability to appreciate others and take risks for oneself are significant parts of this dimension of social interaction.

One child will withdraw from social exchanges, and another child will participate confidently and enthusiastically in these social exchanges. Some children feel comfortable in nonverbal exchanges and others in verbal ones, some in sports but not in intellectual pursuits. The nature of the responsiveness to both adults and peers can be significant in the child's growth and learning.

## Perception

Learning requires the use and integration of the perceptual information processing systems—visual, auditory, and tactile. More or less effective modalities should be noted. Integrative tasks need to be analyzed to determine the child's strengths and weaknesses. Birch and Lefford (1964) present a good strategy for studying perception in children. They stress the importance of intersensory judgment, the relationships between the perceptual modalities, and the need for analysis and synthesis in the perceptual mode. Careful observations of compensatory strategies need to be discovered, explored, and fostered.

The perceptual processing system is a primary mode of intake at the earlier stages of development, and deficits in this function have a profound effect on the child between the ages of four and seven years. Later in the child's development, at age seven and beyond, there is a shift of function to more cognitive processing (Piaget, 1952), which tends to minimize the problem in perceptual processing if the cognitive functions are intact in the child. The child at this later stage tends to pay more attention to the meaning of things rather than to the shape or sound.

For illustration, one child aged five is able to process more effectively in the visual modality while another child may reveal his difficulty in visual perception but shows strength auditorily. Where there is a problem processing in one modality, some compensatory strategy using another may help. In addition, once the child can function cognitively, the meanings (concepts and words) can stabilize the perceptual confusions (Sapir, 1961). More specifically, a child with auditory perceptual confusion might mispronounce the ends of words or may substitute sounds in the medial position (sagetti for spaghetti; when for went) or a child with a visual perceptual problem may not be able to distinguish between a ketchup bottle and a soda bottle in a picture.

### Cognition/Language

This refers to the quality of the child's concepts, the language the child uses, and his understanding of receptive communication. Language can be considered along the following lines: word usage, meaning of words, grammatical structure, symbolic level (concrete to abstract), graphemic and phonemic structures, and the semantics of the language. To explore receptive language, give the child a series of directions to follow, appropriately chosen for the child's age. One can tell a story and ask the child to act it out with puppets. Expressive language can be explored by having the child describe an event or tell a story. Creativity and humor are clues to the child's cognitive ability.

Some children, when faced with a demanding challenge, will avoid the task by distracting or diverting the examiner, using their fine verbal skills. Other language-impaired children may use poor syntax ("He goes where?"), misuse words ("I want a hamburger," when the child wants a frankfurter), difficulty using the same word for different meanings and different parts of speech ("block that kick"; "I live on the *block*"; or "I build with *blocks*"). Another common problem may be the inability to find the target word, as in the case of a child who says, "I went to buy—you know what—you saw it in the store." One is often fooled because such children are very verbal.

### Academic Skills

All the preceding dimensions affect the acquisition of academic skills. A child's ability to listen, speak, read, write, spell, and do arithmetic reflects the distinctive combination of maturation and developmental factors which contribute to his learning potential.

For example, if children remain at a concrete cognitive level in their thinking and have some form of expressive language confusion, it is very difficult for them to understand reading material or to write a story. They can only deal with what they themselves have experienced. Written language is much more difficult than spoken language because it must be more explicit, giving every detail.

Each of the academic skills needs to be explored and understood. The point of breakdown needs to be analyzed in order that the failing tasks can be broken down into smaller chunks that will enable the child to succeed. One sees children who are competent in some academic work and failing in others. This needs to be understood in terms of the nature of the tasks, attitudes toward the content, and interest levels.

## THE USE OF DIMENSIONS AND OBSERVATIONS

To help a learning-disabled child, it is necessary to know what he can and cannot do academically. However, if one tries to concentrate primarily on a hierarchy of learning skills, neglecting the child's temperament, personality, defense against failure, and cognitive style, it is not likely that the child will be motivated or succeed. If one knows, for example, the pace of the child, the child's responsiveness to stimuli, his attention span, the modality in which he does better, and the child's reaction to failure, one can provide a program that will take all these dimensions into account and have some chance for success.

To become competent in observing the dimensions of learning and growth, one should follow certain steps as training methodology. It is necessary to record the observations of the child and state exactly what is happening. It sometimes helps to color code these observations after they have been recorded. A different color for each dimension helps one to single out what the child has done that relates to each dimension. A paragraph describing the child along each dimension is the next step, with a summary statement for each dimension. Last, a form that will allow for a succinct description of the child's strengths and weaknesses in each dimension (see Appendix A) helps one to plan for integrated treatment strategies.*

---

* A videotape, "The Dimensions of Learning: Observing Children," is available from the Indiana Film Library, Bank Street College of Education, or from the author. It was produced by the author, and directed and initiated by Linda Levine and Sergio Rainho at Bank Street College under Grant #G00700944 with U.S. Department of Education, Office of Special Education's Model Programs.

# CHAPTER 6

# Selection
# Procedures

### SELECTION OF CHILDREN

Two critical components of the Clinical Teaching Model are the selection of children and the careful pairing of children and adults as working teams. Children are selected based on observations of them, their families, classmates, and teachers. Observing a family together gives a wealth of information: Who sits next to whom? Who answers the questions raised by the examiner? Do both parents react in the same or different ways to the child? Does one attempt to cuddle the child and the other criticize? Which parent is oversolicitous? Who speaks the most? Who defers to whom?

Depending on the age of the children, tasks may be offered so that they can reveal the child's attempt to solve them. Paper should be available so that children can draw a person with a pencil; crayons can be given to make a picture. Children can be asked to copy the Bender-Gestalt form cards. They can be asked to write their names, words, or sentences depending on age. They can be asked to read some directions written by the examiner and then, after reading them, proceed to follow through on the directions.

The parents' reaction to the child's performance also gives a great deal of insight into the way they deal with the child's problems. Most well-chosen tasks can reveal much information about children, including their understanding of receptive language, ability to relate to other people, awareness of problems, feelings of inadequacy and ways to defend against the feelings, perceptual difficulties, thinking problems, expressive and receptive language problems, temperamental qualities, motivation, cooperativeness, articulation problems, and motor ability.

## Characteristics of the Children to Be Served

The children to be served by the Clinical Teaching Model may cut across all socioeconomic levels and be of diverse racial, ethnic, and cultural backgrounds. Children who fit the description of "Children with Specific Learning Disabilities" (*Federal Register*, February 20, 1975) include

> . . . those children who have a disorder in one or more of the basic psychological processes involved in understanding or in using language, spoken or written, which disorder may manifest itself in imperfect ability to listen, think, speak, read, write, spell, or do mathematical calculations. Such disorders include such conditions as perceptual handicaps, brain injury, minimal brain dysfunction, dyslexia, and developmental aphasia. The term does not include children who have learning problems which are primarily the result of visual, hearing, or motor handicaps, of mental retardation, of emotional disturbance, or of economic disadvantage. (*Federal Register*, February 20, 1975)

It is recognized that within this broad definition of specific learning disabilities there are many different and varied descriptions and characteristics of the children; therefore, no learning-disabled child is just like any other. In the school situation, additional information can be viewed. Does the child relate well to the adult (teacher), and how does that compare to the way the child relates to other children in the class? Does the child seem able to understand what is going on in the class? Does he respond quickly to directions? Is the child paying attention or daydreaming? Does he answer when spoken to? What is his play? How does he respond to motor activities versus desk work activities? If the child shows anxiety, at what tasks does it become prominent? What is the nature of the academic work, and can he proceed on his own correctly?

Specific learning disability is a variable clinical syndrome which changes with the age of the child. Certain disorders may be evident at one stage of development and be replaced by others at another stage. For example, in one child, at three years there is often delayed or inadequate speech, at five poor visual perception, at seven word-finding and syntactical problems. Probably then, the only accurate and most useful description of the child with specific learning disabilities is one that is specific to that child, i.e., one that considers the child's temperamental and cognitive style, as well as his particular behavior problems in a variety of situations. Each child will present his own unique set of clinical symptoms. It is the number of deviations from the norm and their severity that determine the disposition to specific learning disability. Such a problem is revealed by developmental imbalances within the child. Indeed, the key indication of specific learning disabilities, as opposed to other learning problems, is evidence of wide and seemingly inexplicable variations and fluctuating strengths and weaknesses in the child's functioning.

## Criteria for Selection of Children

The child who meets the criteria for selection must reveal discrepancies ranging from competency to inadequacy in one or more of the perceptual, cognitive, and communication skills. Academic skills *must* be retarded by at least two years in one or more of the specifics of reading, writing, spelling, and arithmetic. These difficulties must be embedded in temperamental characteristics that compound the problems. The additional emotional overlay may or may not be a presenting problem.

Generally, these are the children who have inadequate ability to develop strategies of their own that enable them to organize and process all kinds of information to be coded in a memory system ready for recall when needed.

The following criteria serve as guidelines in selecting children. The children selected will exhibit a combination of many of the criteria or a very serious deficit in perceptual-motor cognition or communication skills.

Academic Achievement
- two or more years below age-appropriate achievement in reading, writing, or spelling.

Cognitive
- poor ability to receive and communicate thoughts
- unable to express themselves, orally or in writing
- incorrect use of words; distortion of grammar
- poor enunciation; slurry speech; twisting of syllables
- poor ability to follow directions
- poor ability to process and store information
- poor ability to appreciate age-appropriate jokes

Behavior
- disorganized
- unable to find things on paper, in space, in desks
- unable to sort things out in the environment (where to go for what)
- lack of focus (attentional skills)
- cannot find something on a page
- cannot attend to something once focused (distractibility)
- concentration limited—sometimes perseverative
- low frustration tolerance; gives up easily (says "I don't know;" gives any answer at all)
- impulsive response to tasks (begins to process even
- before entire task is presented)

Perceptual Motor
- poor coordination, particularly in small motor activity
- emotionally labile
- poor visual, auditory, or tactile perception

- poor integration inter- and intra-sensorially
- temporal sequencing auditory problem
- visual sequencing problem

## Example Descriptions of Children

The following describes two children who would fit the criteria for selection.

*Matthew.* Matthew, age six, was referred because he was unable to complete the simplest tasks, had difficulty communicating even the simplest ideas, and seemed unable to understand what was expected of him. He could neither read nor write, spell nor do arithmetical computation.

Temperamentally, he was vulnerable to stress, hyperactive, impulsive, and unpredictable in his behavior and responses to tasks. He seemed unable to complete the simplest perceptual-motor tasks: matching visual, auditory, or kinesthetic stimuli. He tended to be more motor and kinesthetically oriented, and was overstimulated by visual stimuli, unable to sort things out. His spoken language was inaccurate and poorly enunciated so that it was difficult to understand what he was saying. Shown the picture of a flag and asked what it was called, he said, "You know, you know—outside the school—you know," and then he began to sing, "Oh, say can you see." He was unable to organize himself, his space, and his materials.

Emotionally, he was withdrawn, unable to relate, dependent but yet avoiding. He responded to warmth in an overcharged way with an overflow of meaningless words. He was unclear as to what he wanted for himself and the world in which he lived. Matthew was selected because of his many neurological defects—unclear speech, distorted language, perceptual problems embedded in temperamental and emotional difficulties—and because of our awareness of his innate brightness in responses to selected stimuli as well as his strong motivation to succeed.

*Peter.* Peter, age seven, was referred because he was unable to learn the letter names, do arithmetic computation, write, or complete the simplest academic tasks. He was withdrawn and unrelated to the children and adults around him.

Temperamentally, he gave up easily, showed little energy, and revealed a slow reaction time to external stimuli. He was vulnerable to stress and attempted to cope by a rigid response.

He was able to perform most of the perceptual-motor tasks except for the higher levels of sequencing and temporalizing, but mother and school shared with us that he had just achieved this competence, although somewhat delayed. Concepts and thinking processes were good, and he revealed that he knew what he wanted to say but was unable to find the words so that he could be understood. He went into a rage because he would ask for a pencil when he really wanted a crayon.

Peter's emotional development was poor. He was unable to maintain eye contact or share his feelings and needs. He was passive in most of his responses and was slow to be able to proceed in any activity. He was selected as a child with a learning disability because he had advanced thinking processes, subtle but distinctive expressive language deficits, and emotional and temperamental problems that added to his difficulty.

## PAIRING OF TUTORS AND CHILDREN

It is recommended that one compensate for the child's area of deficits with the tutor's strengths. The child will use the tutor's strengths to further the treatment alliance in the same way that the adult uses strengths he or she possesses.

The balancing of tutor with child is based on the tutor's temperament, personality, learning style, clarity of verbalization, and needs. The first step in the process requires that the tutors write an essay on those aspects of their social and cultural backgrounds that influenced them to be the kind of person they are today. This essay, combined with their presentation in the program, enables the staff to rate the tutors on the above-mentioned characteristics. In addition, tutors are asked to state the kind of child they wish to work with, indicating age, sex, personality, learning problem, and style. Also considered is the goal for each of the tutors and the level of their experience.

Because of the belief that the adult tutor needs to make an important commitment to the child, the tutor is given a choice of students who fit the criteria, and she makes the final selection. Thus, the commitment is enhanced. Nevertheless, the match is always based on the child's learning problem, age, personality, cognitive, style, and academic performance as it matches the needs of the adult.

*Criteria for Pairing of Tutors and Children*

The following criteria for pairing are examples of some characteristics that are considered valid for pairing purposes. As noted, they can run from child to adult or vice versa. They seem to enhance the mutual reciprocal influences in the formation of a treatment alliance. They take the form of providing a compensatory balance between tutor and child but apply only to the child's deficits.

Criteria for Pairing

| Child | Adult |
| --- | --- |
| *Temperament* | |
| Slow or fast pace | Moderate-paced |
| Low response to stimuli | Moderate stimuli |
| Impulsive | Reflective |
| Distractible | Focused |
| Gives up easily | Perseveres |
| Rigid | Flexible |
| *Personality (Affect)* | |
| Low self-esteem | High |
| Overcontrolled, compulsive | Expansive |
| Feisty, testing, manipulative | Accepting |
| Denying, negative, or intrusive | Honest and allows for initiative |
| Disorganized | Organized |
| Nonadaptive | Adaptive |
| Stereotypic | Innovative |

| Lack of clarity in verbalization, words, syntax | Clarity and appropriateness of words and syntax |
| Concrete thinking low levels of concepts | Using appropriate levels with developmental pressure to higher level |

## *Examples of Adult Tutor Essays*

Examples of the tutor's essay used to understand the adult tutors before pairing follow.

*Michael.* In his essay Michael writes,

Education was very important. It was a very competitive and regimental system. During that time I remember six different schools which I attended. For me, academically, it was a very uncohesive period. My father had left my mother and me in Cuba while he chased the American dream up-North. Both my mother's and father's family were large. . . . It was they and my mother's occasional employment that sustained us for three years until paper and means were ready for us to rejoin my father in the United States. I suspect that this transiency had its toll on all of us, but for a child in that stage of development, all that disorganization could have had no good effects, or could it?

My childhood was a happy one. The chaos had its reason and was temporary. The varied experiences served me well and I had the opportunity to meet family. At some points, it was rural and slow-moving and, at others, urban and hurried. I experienced flocks of chickens around me with their chicks and eggs and the early rising; the leading of cattle to the slaughter and their butchering; the fishing with my grandfather; the feasts of the Christmas season; the Catholic school; the Methodist school. In the capital with my Aunt Victoria, her husband, and two university sons, I worked and played in their bakery which was full of adventure. The public school there had children of all ages in first grade. The young sat in front. Some were 15 and 16 years old back there, but there seemed to be no problem with that. The revolution was vivid to me in 1958. My cousins went to the hills to join the revolutionary forces, and I remember playing with a real pistol. Life was a textbook.

When I arrived in New York, I was 10 years old and the indoor life began. Television was not only entertainment but a source of knowledge. A good deal of my English was learned there. My first experience in school was very strange. In those days, a person such as myself was still a novelty—someone who couldn't speak English. It was sink or assimilate. I was to go to the fourth grade, but was told I must repeat the third grade since I couldn't speak the language. That seemed very unfair. I had to prove them wrong. By the fourth grade I was writing and reading in English. I was and am very proud of my accomplishments.

Although I couldn't receive any academic help at home, I had a good support system which provided all the physical and emotional necessities to my academic success.

The supervisor, based on objective data as well as subjective feelings, rated Michael as follows:

| | |
|---|---|
| Physical: | Strong and well-built |
| Temperament: | Reflective, open, and well paced |
| Personality: | Optimistic and a fighter; strong ego |
| Language: | Poetic, rhythmic, and excellent |
| Basic Skills: | Good |

Michael was paired with Gerald, age seven, who was rated as follows:

| | |
|---|---|
| Physical: | Strong and active |
| Temperament: | Impulsive, distractible, unevenly paced, poor attention, and poor concentration |
| Personality: | Manipulative, weak ego, denial as defense |
| Language: | Poor English—spoke to me in Spanish, with a mixture of the two languages |
| Basic Skills: | Non-reader, poor math skills, barely able to write name, low concepts |

*Elaine.* In her essay, Elaine writes,

I grew up in the Bronx. My family lived in an apartment in a nonprofit cooperative for lower-middle or working class income groups. The cooperative had its own nursery school and sponsored many activities. People in the community were predominantly Jewish and garment industry workers. People expressed their Jewishness through the history, holiday songs, and the learning of Yiddish at a Jewish school, after regular school.

I am the third of four children. My father came to the U.S. when he was 20. My mother was born here, but her older sisters were born in Europe. My mother was 40 when I was born.

Academics were always stressed. It was assumed that each one of us would go to college—a city college. The game plan for the girls was to go to college, get married, teach (so you have your summers off), and then have children.

My mother and father always wanted me to teach. I didn't know if any other avenues were open to girls. My sister, brother, and brother-in-law all taught. I imagine it was assumed that I would work after marriage. Although my mother may have worked after she was married, she at no time worked while we were growing up. I always knew that I wasn't going to sit at home.

As a child in school, I had difficulty with reading. I never remembered enjoying reading until the seventh grade. My elementary years were disrupted by my mother's illness and two years of problems within the school. One year I had a string of substitutes after the regular teacher left in October. Another year, my teacher had a nervous breakdown and was literally led away from the classroom by another teacher.

I was always quiet, never calling attention to myself. At age 12, I started going away for the summers to a Jewish cultural camp where there was little competition. I thrived there, enjoying sports, music, dance. I was exposed to ballet, classical music, literature, and the politics of the day. Camp was especially important to me because of my mother's illness at home. I was able to escape from some of the responsibilities and realities of home.

I still see myself as quiet, although I make a great effort to overcome it. If I am in a new situation, it usually takes me a while to feel comfortable. I also tend to doubt my own ability, and I have been working on this. I am beginning to trust my instincts more. I am beginning to accept myself as someone who has some worth.

Elaine was rated as follows by her supervisor:

Physical:       Well-built, thin, well-coordinated
Temperament:    Quiet, needs time to adapt; reflective with good
                concentration

| Personality: | A little insecure, timid; not afraid to take a risk |
| Language: | Excellent expressive language |
| Basic Skills: | Had difficulty with reading, but overcame it; writes and reads well now |

She was paired with Mary, ten years of age, with the following characteristics:

| Physical: | Poorly coordinated |
| Temperament: | Impulsive, active, poor attention span |
| Personality: | Denying and afraid to take a risk; tries to manipulate to easier tasks |
| Language: | Word-finding, syntactical, and vocabulary problems |
| Basic Skills: | Poor reading, poor decoding skills; difficulty in handwriting and all writing skills, spelling, grammar and punctuation |

# CHAPTER 7

# A Research Project: Principles of Interaction

---

The Clinical Teaching Model expounded here is complex and has many components. Basic to its many tenets is the importance of the quality of interaction between tutor and child, and the integration of this interaction with other components of the system and particularly with cognitive enhancement. With the belief that the interaction between tutor and child is of vital importance, an investigation of the validity of this principle was begun. A search was undertaken for research investigating variables such as pairing adults (tutors, teachers, psychotherapists, or counselors) with children (students, clients), interpersonal compatibility in adult-child dyads, academic achievement, performance, and self-enhancement. Although there are data available on group interactions, little has been investigated on the effect of interactions and reciprocal influences upon the adult and child in a cognitive and/or therapeutic exchange.

## RESEARCH ON A "MATCHING PRINCIPLE"

Wetzel, Schwartz, and Vasu (1979), as well as Maves (1983), investigated college roommate compatibility. Wetzel et al., supported by Maves, concluded that the "similarity" hypothesis of interpersonal attraction (that one is attracted to and compatible with people who have similar self-concepts) received moderate support; the "social desirability" hypothesis (that one is attracted to and compatible with people who possess socially desirable traits) received scant support; the "ideal" hypothesis (that one is attracted to and compatible with people who are similar to one's ideals) received strong support.

Another approach studied the effects of cognitive style matching with 32 student-teacher pairs (Packer & Bain, 1978). In this study teachers and students were matched or mismatched on one of two cognitive style dimensions: serialism/holism and field dependence/independence. Teachers taught their partners a 30-40 minute lesson on the mathematical concept network tracing. Matching effects proved significant in developing mathematical concepts. Kaufman (1979) studied the match and mismatch of cognitive styles in vocational counseling. He found a relationship between these cognitive style matches and the effectiveness of the vocational counseling process.

Although none of these studies have direct applicability to the proposed study, some interesting observations may be noted. The "ideal" hypothesis seems to have the most support in the Wetzel et al. study. The significance of the cognitive match in the Packer and Bain, and Kaufman investigations lends some support to the notion that "matching," in principle, may have some validity.

Therapist-client dyads examined the characteristics of members of the dyad and their relationship to outcome. In a study of client-counselor similarity and counseling outcome, Peters (1980) found that in a juvenile diversion program, counselors' and clients' similar characteristics influenced the outcome in clients. Stern (1979), in a study of interpersonal compatibility and counseling supervision, found that the quality and outcome of supervision were related to the level of interpersonal compatibility. Malloy (1981) confirmed that there was a significant relationship between the therapist-client interpersonal compatibility, the sex of the therapist, and the psychotherapeutic outcome. Norman (1977), investigating relationships in the counseling dyad, found correlations between attitude similarity, interpersonal compatibility, and the progress made in the psychotherapeutic process. Hurst (1979) found a relationship between client satisfaction and progress, and similarities of counselor-client interpersonal values. It is of note that all the above studies are of adult dyads, and caution must be exercised to apply the findings to an adult-child dyad. Nevertheless, there appears to be a relationship between certain characteristics of the professional and client that has an effect on the outcome of the treatment. It is possible that this generalization may be applied to the adult-child dyad.

A few studies attempted to link interaction and personal compatibility with cognitive achievement in adults. Brown (1978) studied the effects of congruency between learning style and teaching style on college students' achievement. He found that college student learners enter a learning situation with a preconceived notion of what teaching style is best for them. For those subjects perceiving congruency between their preferred style and the teaching style actually practiced, achievement was greater than for those perceiving incongruency. He concluded that this has implications for teacher effectiveness and outcomes. Fry and Charron (1980) investigated the effects of cognitive style and counselor-client compatibility on client growth. They concluded that growth was related to the ease of the communication between counselor and client. They urged a person-environment interaction model to achieve maximum counselor-client compatibility and client growth. Blackmer (1981) studied the contribution made to student achievement by the degree of cognitive style match between peer tutors and college students and found a positive relationship. Newton (1981) investigated and found that in a dyad the relationship context and compatibility had an impact on the effectiveness of the communication system.

Thomas, Ribich, and Freie (1982) found that college students who identify highly with their instructors rate courses more favorably and perceive greater progress on their part toward course-related objectives. Gates (1978), in an exploratory study, found that student teachers and their cooperating teachers' characteristics were related to the degree of student teacher success. Paul (1973) showed that student-teacher compatibility affected students' achievement outcome in algebra. In a study of the outcome of speech therapy with stutterers, McClintock (1979) found that, the more positive the therapeutic relationship, the greater the decrease in stuttering. Carr and Posthuma (1975), focusing on patient-therapist and student-teacher dyads, investigated the role of cognitive processes in social interaction. Patient-therapist cognitive compatibility was shown to predict treatment success whereas the instructor's cognitive organizational structure was of more importance in the educational relationship. Moras and Strupp (1982) found that the assessments of interpersonal relations to form a treatment alliance in a therapist-client dyad correlated with outcomes at a modest level.

There were a few studies dealing with adult-child interactions and performance outcomes. Collins (1970) investigated the influence of interpersonal compatibility on fourth and sixth grade pupils' mathematics and social studies achievement by looking at the teachers' and pupils' perceptions of the relationship. They found that, the more positive the perceptions of the relationship, the higher the achievement. Schultz (1972) investigated the influence of teacher behavior and dyad compatibility on clinical gains in arithmetic tutoring with learning-disabled students. He studied the independent and combined influence of teacher facilitative behavior (empathy and interpersonal respect) and interpersonal compatibility between teacher and student on selected arithmetic educational outcomes. The results of analysis of variance procedures failed to support hypothesized relationships between teacher facilitative behavior, interpersonal compatibility, and many of the dependent variables.

Gourevitch (1982), writing on "Encounter and Communication," stressed the importance of interaction and reciprocal influence. She discussed how an individual can have a genuine encounter with another person and be moved deeply by it without feeling the need or possessing the ability to articulate the bond in logical and consciously chosen terms. Such a contact creates the conditions for mutual understanding and a feeling of enrichment, and she believes that such an encounter leads to growth and the development of one's potential.

## THE PROJECT: RECIPROCAL INFLUENCES IN A TREATMENT ALLIANCE

This project was designed to study the nature of the interaction between graduate-student tutors and learning-disabled children working together in a practicum training program. It consists of a study of dyads (tutors and children) previously videotaped in Bank Street College's Learning Disability Laboratory, a Child Service Demonstration Center. The study ran for a period of three years (1977-1980) and was funded by the Bureau of the Educationally Handicapped Model Programs. It examines the development of a treatment alliance between the tutor and the child through a planned match of the members of the dyad. A mutually responsive verbal and nonverbal communication system was investigated in order to assess the effect of the quality of this treatment alliance on the social, emotional, and cognitive growth of both tutor and child. Prior to this study, the progress of the child and graduate-student tutor had been categorized by the supervisor as either minimal, average, or excellent. These data were then correlated with the number of positive and negative interactions (the treatment alliance) by measuring movement, facial expressions, and verbalizations in both tutor and child.

Based on the assumption that good reciprocal pairing of tutor and child is critical to the growth of an effective treatment alliance, characteristics of both tutor and child were examined along specific dimensions (temperament, personality, cognition, style, and clarity of verbalization) in an attempt to determine which characteristics in the tutor mesh best with which characteristics in the child to foster the formation of a treatment alliance. The verbal and nonverbal communication system of the dyad was assessed to determine if a treatment alliance had developed.

While the number of children with learning disabilities is growing in epidemic proportions (Silverman, 1982), treatment methods practiced in our schools are questioned because they have produced minimal results. One possibility may be that the emphasis on cognitive intervention, although essential, needs to be placed into a different framework. Research should be devoted to identifying those factors that contribute to successful therapeutic outcomes and enhance the development of strategies for effective learning and growth in learning-disabled children.

This study is based on the belief that the quality of the match between the teacher and the child, and the treatment alliance that subsequently develops, may be the key that provides access to children's reservoir of abilities allowing for their change and growth. This might be a factor leading to success in all types of treatment models. It may be possible to approach the treatment of learning-disabled, handicapped children from the perspective of the dynamics of the tutor-child match, the communication system between the members of the dyad, and the treatment alliance that develops as they work together cognitively and effectively.

Because so many learning-disabled children have experienced so much failure and feel so chronically inadequate, they are resistant to learning. Disruptive or passive behavior is a manifestation of their attempts to hide a sense of personal inadequacy, making it almost impossible for teachers or resource personnel to reach them through conventional teaching methods. Only with the development of a relationship of responsivity based on a shared understanding of the child's plight and its reciprocal effect on the adult may it be possible for any change to take place. For the child, this change may be reflected in many ways, including increased energy available for learning; a positive change in behavior; an ability to socialize in more appropriate ways; a willingness to try new ways; increased ability to express and share feelings and needs; a greater feeling of optimism in approaching a problem; and increased feelings of independence and personal competence. For the adult, the change may involve the development of insights into the child's feelings; the satisfaction of seeing how feedback engenders enhanced self-esteem; the awareness that success need not depend on negative means of control; learning more about children's communication systems; and the awareness of one's own motivations, attitudes, and communication style.

The importance of the treatment alliance came to the surface repeatedly in many ways in the course of the three-year model program. For example, many parents of learning-disabled children reported that they had had similar learning-disability problems. When asked how they had overcome their problems, they always told about someone who had understood and helped them, someone with whom they had felt a close relationship, someone who cared about and supported them, and with whom they had formed a treatment alliance.

The nature of the reciprocal interactive process between child and adult can produce a positive or negative feedback system which, in turn, may enhance or inhibit the growth and development of both members of the dyad. Interactions have been described as lying somewhere on a continuum from synchronous/harmonious to disorganized/disturbed (Field, 1978). Both adult and child enter into an interaction with a unique configuration of traits. The match of these unique individual personality traits may be the critical factor in positive feedback systems (Hunt, 1966). Communication is a complex system in which a unit of behavior is both a response of one participant and a stimulus for the other (Glidewell, 1961); the need to analyze this dynamic interactive process has been documented (Bell, 1971, 1979). Developing training guidelines requires a theory and a model of operation of reciprocal influences whereby a tutor can learn how to anticipate and respond to a child's communication in the efforts to try to foster the development of an alliance (Bell, 1971, 1979; Brazelton, 1979; Field, 1978; Fraiberg, 1974; Glidewell, 1961; Harper, 1971; Hunt, 1966; Lewis, 1974; Rosenblum & Youngstein, 1974; Yarrow, Waxler, & Scott, 1971).

Research on these relationships, especially in therapeutic situations, becomes very difficult, particularly when the focus is on the interconnections between the individuals rather than on the usual patterns of cause and effect. Penman (1980), in taking a hard look at communication systems, rejects notions of independent and dependent variables and suggests instead an emphasis on interdependence and organization. Rather than seeking basic elements and static entities, one should focus on contextual hierarchical structures and fluctuating processes; instead of trying to discover laws of behavior, the objective is to understand human rules of action. There has been some research on communication and relationships as ongoing processes, employing methods appropriate to a systems framework, exemplified by John Gottman's (1979) study of sequential action and reciprocal behavior.

Penman (1980) addresses issues of explicit and implicit aspects of messages, using a two-dimensional scheme in which messages are coded in terms of power and involvement. Her research involved 18 couples whose relationships ranged in length from one to 33 years. Tape recordings were made of the couples discussing three different items over a 60-minute period. Some interesting findings are pertinent to this research. Incongruities between implicit and explicit levels occur for all couples. Sequential dependencies in messages are generally based on the other's immediately antecedent action, but not always. For a substantial minority of participants, constraint derives from their own prior message. Thus, in some instances, noninteraction can characterize the communication process, and Penman suggests that such responses to "self" reflect interactions biased by individuals' internal predictions and goals. This finding has particular significance for the present study in light of the importance of the child's self-concept and anticipation of either success or failure. This may determine the child's accessibility to intervention.

Research also supports the concept of the importance of individual personality traits and the reciprocal nature of the relationship between therapist and child. Bates and Pettit (1981) discuss adult individual differences as moderators of child effects. Building on Bell's (1971) crystallization of the child effects notion, models of social development have increasingly emphasized the child as an active agent in the socialization process. Well-controlled research (Barkley, 1981; Chapman, 1981) has shown that specific child behaviors can affect an average adult in ways that have relevance to the child's development. The assumption that adult individual differences can moderate the behavior of children is supported by the literature, as is the converse, the child's influence on the adult. As questions and methods become refined, such work will eventually provide a more generalized view of the reciprocal quality of the interactions between adults and children.

There are many variables that might affect child and adult behavior and communication systems including, for example, cultural differences, social class, adult depression, and nurturance patterns. Particular child or adult characteristics will not be equally germane to all possible interaction situations. The challenging issue of choice of adult, child, and situational variables for study is a crucial aspect of this project.

## Definition of Terms

A *treatment alliance* for the purpose of this study is defined operationally as:

1) the precise match of an adult and a child along specific criteria selected from the trait analysis (Scales I and II, see Appendix B and C) of each member of the dyad; and,
2) the mutual responsivity of the members of the dyad that allows each to respond to verbal and nonverbal cues in a positive way (as measured by Scale III, see Appendix D).

*Reciprocal influences* in a dyad are defined operationally as the way one person's communication activates and influences the nature of the response in the other member of the dyad. Each further communication acts as a stimulus for another response which influences the communication process.

*Mutual responsivity* is defined operationally as the response of each member of the dyad to the verbal or nonverbal communication of the other. Each response is a stimulus for another response which then becomes the stimulus for yet another communicative response.

*Positive responses* are defined operationally as:

1) movement toward the other member of the dyad;
2) facial expression of pleasure (smiling, excitement, pleasurable eye contact); and
3) verbal expressions of pleasure, support, or empathy.

*Negative responses* are defined operationally as:

1) movement away from the other member of the dyad;
2) facial expression of dissatisfaction (grimacing, puzzlement, dismay, a general expression of displeasure); and

3) verbal expressions conveying negativism (hostility, manipulation, denials).

*Hypothesis*

The hypothesis of this project is as follows:

1) A careful reciprocal pairing between the personality (affect), temperament, and cognitive style of the tutor and the learning-disabled child is a key to ensuring a continuous, harmonious feedback system that will promote the growth of a treatment alliance.
2) Once the reciprocal pairing is correct, selected behaviors in the interaction, as planned and deliberately carried out by the tutor, are critical to the development of a treatment alliance.
3) The ability of the tutor and child to discover together the nuances of their reciprocal exchanges and to communicate them to each other is vital to the development of a treatment alliance.
4) The tutor-child interactive system is facilitated by mutual responsivity and continuous modification of responses.
5) A treatment alliance is an important factor in the learning and growth of each member of the dyad.

The study included the following:

• Refinement and application of observational system using scales for measuring individual characteristics of tutor and child, and the communication system between them.
• Determination of which characteristics in children and adults can predict the formation of an effective match, as measured by the verbal and nonverbal communications and the progress of the children;
• Determination of what attributes go into the mutual responsivity that allows for the development of the treatment alliance.

## Subjects

Learning-disabled children, ages four to 12, from the inner-city public schools were selected for tutorial treatment in the Learning Disability Lab of Bank Street College. Because this is a training model, the child population is diverse in many respects: ethnicity, socioeconomic status, and complexity of problems.

The majority of the graduate-student tutors are in training for a Masters Degree or Professional Diploma in Special Education, Supervision, or Administration. They have completed study in normal and deviant child development, and methodology of treatment, and have had fieldwork in clinical and educational settings.

The subject units of the pilot study were five graduate student (tutor)-child dyads previously videotaped during the three-year Learning Disability Laboratory Project. Prior to the collection of data, the progress of both the graduate student and the child in each dyad was entered into one of three categories (Excellent, Average, Minimal Progress). These categories were based on reports from two sources for the tutors (an instructor in the project, and supervisors of the graduate students), and three sources for the children (parents, childrens' classroom teachers, and supervisors in the project). Determination of the appropriate category based on these reports was made by two independent observers: 1) the researcher of the project and 2) an outside evaluator statistician.

## Setting for Videotaping

Each tutor-child dyad had been videotaped at least three times during the year (November/December; February/March; April/May) for not less than 15 minutes. The videotaping took place in a standardized setting. The tutor-child dyad worked in a small, soundproof room. The camera was extended through a hole in the one-way mirror arrangement so that there was no interference from the camera or media personnel. Children and graduate students had become acquainted with the setting, were encouraged to watch taping of others, and were only exposed to videotaping when they felt ready to proceed.

The graduate students worked with their supervisors to plan the activities for the videotaping segments. The work was of a cognitive nature, but sometimes took the form of play activities or games in the development of reading, writing, and math skills. The tasks differed according to the age and need of the child and reflected the child's motivation, attitudes, and interests.

The videotape segments to be analyzed were randomly selected by the media specialist, an independent observer. Without any communication from other members of the research team, the media specialist selected five dyads from 60 one-hour cinéma vérité videotapes produced during the three years of the Learning Disability Lab's functioning. Randomly selected sequences of two minutes each from the hour-long tapes of the graduate student and child working together were selected. The numbers of the playback machine and the first and last words in the segment were recorded. Tapes of just those selected sequences were then made so that there was ready access for coding by the researchers.

## Measures

A search was made to find any standardized tests available to study the interactive communication in a tutor-child dyad, but this proved quite limiting. The only test found in the literature was Schutz's Fundamental Interpersonal Relations Orientations Scales Behavior (FIRO-B) (1967), used with adults only. Frandsen and Rosenfeld (1973) conducted a series of studies with college students and civil service employees to investigate the potential usefulness of Schutz's theory of interpersonal relations orientations for the study of communication in dyads. Based on an analysis of the descriptive and exploratory power of scores produced by responses to Schutz's instrument, the three-dimensional classification of interpersonal needs, as well as the three forms of interpersonal compatibility, were challenged. Results suggested that FIRO-B may be structurally biased against the interpersonal need to control or be controlled and that the compatibility measures do not permit analysis of the functional relationship between interpersonal orientations and communicative processes in dyads. Underwood and Krafft (1973) also concluded that Schutz's FIRO-B compatibility theory, based on interpersonal need satisfaction, did not hold in the context of studying the relationship of managerial work effectiveness to interpersonal compatibility.

One of the major activities of this study was the formalization of data-gathering instruments and procedures. Reliability was established through test-retest procedures. Internal consistency studies, in which six graduate students observed and recorded simultaneously, were used to refine and formalize the observational system and measures. Where observations differed, the item was dropped.

The scales used in this project identified the characteristics of adult and child. They tried to determine which of these characteristics were significant in formulating a treatment alliance. Another measure evaluated the interactive quality of the verbal and nonverbal communication system: how messages were received and responded to.

The scales were based on information available in developmental and linguistic literature (Erikson, 1963; Piaget, 1961) but which had not heretofore been translated into reliable, clinically useful procedures for clinicians, special educators, and therapists interested in these problems.

*Development of measures.* The development of the trait analysis scales became an extension of the process of developing an observational guide used to study children in the Learning Disability Laboratory. Seven dimensions were described in the guide, but the most essential dimensions for the purposes of this research were considered to be personality, temperament, and cognitive style and clarity of expression. This choice was based on the theories of Erikson (1963), Chess (1967), Vygotsky (1962), and Piaget (1961). Personality characteristics were based on Erikson's psychosocial stages, temperament on Chess's definitions, and cognitive style and clarity of expression on Piaget's and Vygotsky's theories of language development.

In the development of the trait analysis scales, the traits defined under each of the categories (personality, temperament, and cognitive style and clarity of expression) were sampled, tested, and refined; some items were deleted, others added.

As stated before, a reliable measure had not yet been developed to study interactions between child and adult. Of the many attempts (Lewis & Lee-Painter, 1974) being made to measure the quality of the caregiver-infant dyad and the few (Bates & Pettit, 1981) being made to measure the relationships between tutors and children or therapists and clients, most progress has been made in the study of the caretaker-infant dyad. Greenspan and Liberman (1980) at the National Institute of Health, Lipsitt (1979) at Yale, and Brazelton (1978) at Harvard have been experimenting with caretaker-infant measures that they have developed. While all look promising, they tend to focus on the infant-mother dyad and are very complex and time-consuming instruments which cannot be applied to the tutor-child dyad.

Since an appropriate standardized tool to study the interactions between tutors and children could not be found, a group of experienced special educators volunteered to study the videotapes of graduate student tutor-child dyads working together, as part of the Learning Lab training experience. With the help of the director of the Learning Lab, they developed the three experimental scales that were used in this project.

To report observations of the characteristics of tutors and children, differentiation of levels was necessary. A three-point scale provided too little differentiation while a ten-point scale offered too much. A six-point scale proved to be sufficiently differentiated and observer-reliable, and was then adopted.

The first goal was to see if the results obtained using these scales would prove to be reliable and valid. Inter-observer reliability was established when five graduate students were able to record similar findings. Some concern remained that this resulted from the students' training in the use of our diagnostic process which studies the child along seven dimensions. To test inter-observer reliability, five special educators who had not been trained in our method were asked to code the data to see if they would get similar results. This proved successful in that they achieved 80% similarity; the scale was considered to be reliable. The issue of consistency was considered later when the scales were applied to sequences of the same dyad videotaped at different times to see if the personal traits data held over time, and they did. Validity of the trait analysis scales were verified through other data (biographies of tutors, supervisors' descriptions of tutors and children, research data; see following chapters for case studies) collected during the three years of the model program. It has been established that they do test what they are intended to test. Therefore, the two trait analysis measures were considered to be reliable, consistent, and valid, although further refinement and experimentation are encouraged.

The third measure developed to record the interactive communication system between the graduate-student tutor and the child proved more difficult. After attempts to record at the same time all that was happening on the tape, the focus was narrowed to recording of movement, facial expression, and verbalization. An original plan to record positive ( + ) and negative ( − ) responses plus distraction (d) and puzzlement (p) was abandoned when it became evident that this was an unrealistic task. For example, a child at the same given moment might move away from the adult, make a face, and say some words. It was decided that each variable would have to be recorded separately by reviewing the tape three times, once for each variable. Through trial and error, a decision was made to record in the following order.

1) movement (without sound)
2) facial expressions (without sound)
3) verbalizations (with sound and vision)

As more experimentation proceeded, it was felt that the distraction and puzzlement offered little additional information, and it was decided to record them as negative ( − ).

Time was spent discussing and trying different ways to record data that allowed an understanding of time sequence—what came first, who responded to what, when a pause or a change of communication occurred. This was a very important issue and one that was critical to understanding the nature of the interactive data: What was the stimulus and was there a response or a change of topic? Again, after much trial and error, it was decided that the record sheets would be lined and that each line would represent a communication in time in the order in which the exchange occurred. If there was a pause, a line would be skipped. If the communication was shifted or changed in any way, a line would also be skipped to so indicate. It was felt that this would allow us to look at the data to see if communication was of an interactive quality.

Next, selection of tapes and the length of the sequence that would be most effective were considered. It was decided that the media specialist should select the tapes at random, providing a random sample of dyads to be studied. After several trials, a three-minute segment was found to be long enough to give good evidence of the interaction and short enough to be manageable. With the help of the media specialist, approximately 25 numbers on the video playback machine were selected as the length of the sequence to be viewed three times, twice without sound for recording of facial expressions and movements, and once with sound for the recording of verbal communications. The record forms for the collection of data would hold the following information for each dyad being studied: the first names of the pair dyad; the beginning and end number of the sequence; and the first words and last words of the sequence to verify the beginning and end of the sequence and allow for differences in the recording of numbers on the playback machine as a result of the way the feeder was threaded.

Each characteristic of the child or tutor was recorded on a 0 to 5 scale, from the weakest to the strongest as viewed on the videotape. Two and 3 are seen as average; 0 to 1 indicates an area of problem, and 4 or 5 indicates strength. As examples:

- A child who is so impulsive that he begins the task before the instructions are given would be rated 0 on the impulsive-reflective item, while a child who waits patiently, listens, and asks a question to be sure before he proceeds would then be rated 5.
- a tutor who asks a child to write a sentence and in the middle of the task asks the child to write a word or look at a picture would be rated 1 on the fragmented-organized item.
- A child who jumps up from his chair and moves about the room and looks up when he hears noises from outside the room would be rated 1 in arbitrary control and 1 in distractibility.

*Recording of interactive processes.* Because cognitive tasks are ongoing, responses to the tutor's cognitive stimulus were not recorded. The data recorded related to mutual responsivity and negative and positive reinforcers through verbalizations (words), facial expressions, and body movement. They were recorded as follows:

| Verbalization | V |
| Facial expression | F |
| Body movement | M |

Each response was also recorded as either positive ( + ) or negative ( − ) (to include puzzlement or distraction). Each recording was placed on a separate line. For example:

| Child smiles | F+ |
| Adult pats child | M+ |
| Child looks puzzled | F− |
| Child is distracted (looks away) | M− |
| "You are doing a good job" | V+ |
| Adult says, "Don't do that!" | V− |

Cognitive questions requiring a direct factual answer from the child were not recorded. Coded responses were reinforcers, clarification questions asked by the child or adult, and verbalizations with emotional intent. Examples of adult responses coded are: "That's good," "If you try you often get the response," "Keep up the good work." Child responses included: "Help me as you did yesterday," "I hope I get them today as I did yesterday," "Sit next to me," "I never get it right," "I have so much trouble with. . . ."

The lines in the interactional tool represent the time sequence so that it is possible to observe responsiveness as follows:

- adult behavior followed by child's positive or negative responses;
- child behavior followed by adult's positive or negative responses;
- responses from either child or adult that became stimuli for further interaction.

Where there is no responsiveness, a line is skipped. Of special interest was the interactive nature of the relationship between adult and child. Did they respond to verbal or nonverbal communication? What was the ratio of positive to negative responses. In which of the modes of communication were there more positive responses?

The interactive measures were recorded as follows:

1) The number of positive responses in each of the three modes (facial, movement, or verbalization) was recorded for each member of the dyad.

2) The number of negative responses in each mode was recorded.

3) The number of negative interactions was subtracted from the number of positive interactions. (It would be possible for an individual to have equal numbers of positive and negative responses which would affect the interactions by neutralizing the positive responses).

4) Interactive responses were totaled separately for facial expressions, movement responses, and verbalizations, thus allowing the researchers to see the relationship of communication in these three different expressive modes. This turned out to be an additional way to determine the adult and child's primary mode of communication.

5) In cases where the interactive communication became the stimuli for another round of interactions, an additional positive response was added for that interaction.

6) Criteria were established to categorize the final interactive response rating, as follows:

> excellent—above 70% interactive
> average—40% to 70% interactive
> poor—below 40% interactive

7) Comparisons of the analysis of interaction in each dyad with the earlier rating of child and tutor progress based on prior recorded data were correlated and scores obtained.

*Coding personnel selection and training.* Three graduate students who had completed the special education practicum programs were selected to serve as coders. These students were not involved in any other aspects of the program. They followed strict time allocations, and adhered to a strict time schedule so that the data were collected over a short timespan of one month.

The director of the project trained the graduate students in the coding of the scales. In order to establish reliability of training procedures, the trainees who did the coding must have reached a specific degree of agreement (80%) with the trainer (director of the project) before they were given the data to code. Training continued until the results obtained from viewing the same videotape segment reached 80% reliability among the three coders.

*Reliability issues.* Reliability was established with 80% agreement on all items. Those items that did not attain 80% agreement were dropped, and adjustments made in the scale to reflect these differences. To prevent bias, the coding personnel did not know either member of the dyad. Every effort was made to keep information confidential.

Because the reliability seemed quite good on most coded items, questions were raised as to whether this might be a result of the type of training these students had received at Bank Street College. With this in mind, three additional observers who had had no previous contact with Bank Street College coded two of the tape segments; in this case, too, it was shown to be 80% reliable.

Then, for each dyad, three independent observers viewed the randomly selected segments of videotape and recorded observations of each child's personality, temperament, and cognitive style, using the trait analysis of children's characteristics that was developed for this study. This procedure was repeated for the graduate student tutor. The three independent observers then viewed and recorded the communication system of interactions of the members of the dyad (graduate student tutor-child) using the same short videotape segments. Observations were recorded using the mutual responsivity scale developed for this study as follows:

- positive and negative facial expressions (recorded without sound when viewing videotapes);
- positive and negative movement (recorded without sound when viewing videotapes);
- positive and negative verbalizations (recorded with sound when viewing videotapes).

## Analysis

The data were analyzed as follows:

1) Correlation of trait analysis pairing to the number of interactive responses in each dyad.

2) Correlation of the interactions between tutor and child with the prior categorization of the progress of the child and tutor.

## 1) Trait Analysis Pairing

The results of the trait analysis data are as follows:

*Carol (tutor) and Billy (child):* original pairing based on cognitive style, personality, and temperament. The data confirmed the pairing on the following traits:

| Trait | Adult | Child |
|---|---|---|
| Personality | Strong ego | Weaker ego |
| | Supportive and emphatic | Low frustration tolerance |
| Temperament | Reflective | Impulsive |
| | Moderate pace | Slow pace |
| | Persevering | Distractible |
| Cognitive Style | Organized | Fragmented |
| | Clarity of verbalizations | Poor verbal expressiveness |
| | Clarity of concepts | Poor understanding of concepts |

(42%)—Eight traits out of 19 recorded were well paired on the original criteria.

*Joan (tutor) and Tony (child):* original pairing based on cognitive style, personality, and temperament. The data confirmed the pairing on the following traits:

| Trait | Adult | Child |
|---|---|---|
| Personality | Moderate ego | Weak ego |
| | Assertive | Lacking in assertiveness |
| Temperament | Focused | Poor attention |
| Cognitive Style | Organized | Fragmented |
| | Clarity of verbalizations | Poor verbalization |
| | Clarity of concepts | Poor concepts |

(32%)  Six traits out of a possible 19 traits recorded were well paired on the original criteria.

*Barbara (tutor) and Thomas (child):* original pairing based on high level of verbalization and intellectualization as well as personality and temperament. The data confirmed the pairing on the following traits:

| Trait | Adult | Child |
|---|---|---|
| Personality | Strong ego | Weaker ego |
| | Excellent frustration tolerance | Poor frustration tolerance |
| Temperament | Focused | Poor attention |
| | Reflective | Impulsive |
| Cognitive Style | Organized | Disorganized |

(26%)—Five traits of 19 recorded were well paired on the original criteria.

*Peg (tutor) and Alfred (child):* original pairing based on personality, temperament and cognitive style. The data confirmed the pairing on the following traits:

| Trait | Adult | Child |
|---|---|---|
| Personality | Strong ego | Weak ego |
| | Excellent frustration tolerance | Poor frustration tolerance |
| Temperament | Focused | Poor attention |
| | Persevering | Non-perseverance |
| | Reflective | Impulsive |
| Cognitive Style | Organized | Disorganized |
| | Clarity of verbalization | Poor verbalization |
| | Clarity of concepts | Poor concepts |

(42%)—Eight traits of 19 recorded were well paired by original criteria.

## Summary of Trait Analysis Pairing

Both the Carol and Billy, and Peg and Alfred dyads recorded eight traits out of 19 that were well paired on predetermined criteria for pairing tutors and children. Joan and Tony recorded six traits well paired, while Barbara and Thomas had five traits well paired.

The results of the progress of the tutors and children in the five dyads had previously been recorded based on the instructor's and supervisor's judgment of the progress of the tutors and children. Standardized tests previously administered to the children were compared and verified the instructor's and supervisor's judgments. Interestingly, although the data for the tutors were recorded separately from the data of the children's progress, in all cases the tutor and child fell within the same category as follows:

| | |
|---|---|
| Barbara and Thomas | Excellent Progress |
| Carol and Billy | Excellent Progress |
| Peg and Alfred | Fair Progress |
| Joan and Tony | Poor Progress |

The five video segments were of three-minute duration for each of the dyads. There were two different segments of Carol and Billy, made at different periods of time, which made it possible to test the reliability of using such a short video segment as a meaningful exchange between adult and child, and to determine whether these communication patterns persist over time.

## 2) Interactions Between Tutor and Child

The findings reveal the number of interactions related to total recorded responses.

*Carol and Billy*
Sequence No. 1              78% interactive (average 6.7 interactive responses out of a total of 8.5)
66% responsive to child's communication

*Carol and Billy*
Sequence No. 2              84% interactive (average 8.9 interactive out of a total of 10.6)
78% responsive to child's communication

*Barbara and Thomas*       68% interactive (9.3 interactive responses out of a total of 13.5)
58% responsive to child's communication

| | |
|---|---|
| *Peg and Alfred* | 52% interactive (5.0 interactive responses out of a total of 9.5) |
| | 40% responsive to child's communication |
| *Joan and Tony* | 38% interactive (2.5 interactive responses out of a total of 6.5) |
| | 31% responsive to child's communication |

The results of the analysis of trait match to interactive responses with prior recorded progress outcome are as follows:

| | Trait Match | Interactive | Progress Outcome |
|---|---|---|---|
| Carol and Billy | 42% | 78% to 84% | Excellent |
| Barbara and Thomas | 26% | 68% | Excellent |
| Peg and Alfred | 42% | 52% | Fair |
| Joan and Tony | 32% | 38% | Poor |

### Summary of Interactions Between Tutor and Child

The hypothesis that a careful pairing between the tutor and the learning-disabled child in personality, temperament, and cognitive style is a key to ensuring a continuous, harmonious feedback system that will promote the growth of a treatment alliance seems not to be confirmed.

However, the interaction hypothesis that a treatment alliance is an important factor in the learning and growth of each member of the dyad does garner support. The relatively high percentage of positive interactive communication (68% and 84%) is associated with the opinions of former recorders, based on the research data collected in the Demonstration Center, that the growth of Barbara and Thomas and Carol and Billy has been excellent.

The percentage of interactions (52%) of a positive nature between Peg and Alfred is within the fair interactive range and is associated with the fair progress of Peg and Alfred. The percentage of positive interactions (38%) in the case of Joan and Tony is poor and is associated with the earlier data of poor progress in both members of the dyad.

## PROFILES OF TUTORS AND CHILDREN

In addition to the above information, profiles were drawn indicating the nature of the interactive responses; how many were movement, how many facial expressions, and how many verbalizations. These provided the following data (counting all communications even when not a response to another):

*Carol and Billy (Sequence I)*

|  | Adult | | Child | |
|  | Positive | Negative | Positive | Negative |
| --- | --- | --- | --- | --- |
| verbal | 6.0 | 0 | 2.5 | 1.0 |
| facial | 2.3 | 0 | 2.0 | 1.3 |
| movement | 1.1 | 0 | 2.5 | 1.3 |

Style of child: some negativism kept to a minimum by style of adult; child uses all forms of communication freely

Style of adult: positive (no negative communication); highly verbal with some facial expression

*Carol and Billy (Sequence II)*

|  | Adult | | Child | |
|  | Positive | Negative | Positive | Negative |
| --- | --- | --- | --- | --- |
| verbal | 7.0 | 0.0 | 5.7 | 1.1 |
| facial | 1.4 | 0.0 | 3.0 | 0.4 |
| movement | 1.7 | 0.0 | 1.0 | 0.9 |

Style of child: style reveals a lessening of movement response and an increase in verbalization

Style of adult: the style of the adult remains constant with emphasis on verbalization

## Barbara and Thomas

| | Adult | | Child | |
|---|---|---|---|---|
| | Positive | Negative | Positive | Negative |
| verbal | 3.0 | 1.1 | 3.1 | 2.1 |
| facial | 3.0 | 0.3 | 5.5 | 1.5 |
| movement | 4.5 | 1.0 | 2.2 | 1.3 |

Style of child: very expressive; very communicative; more positive than negative; communicates primarily with combination of facial expressions and verbalizations

Style of adult: very expressive; very communicative and interactive with emphasis on movement, but much verbalization and facial expression; small percentage of negative responses

## Peg and Alfred

| | Adult | | Child | |
|---|---|---|---|---|
| | Positive | Negative | Positive | Negative |
| verbal | 3.3 | 1.5 | 1.0 | 3.0 |
| facial | 0.1 | 0.0 | 1.0 | 3.0 |
| movement | 1.0 | 0.6 | 1.1 | 3.6 |

Style of child: highly negative with minimal involvement of a positive nature; communicates through verbalization, facial expression, and movement, with slightly more movement responses

Style of adult: little interaction; mostly verbal, but some expressions of negativism

## Joan and Tony

| | Adult | | Child | |
|---|---|---|---|---|
| | Positive | Negative | Positive | Negative |
| verbal | 2.0 | 0.1 | 0.3 | 0.1 |
| facial | 0.3 | 0.0 | 4.0 | 0.6 |
| movement | 2.0 | 0.6 | 2.5 | 0.5 |

Style of child: mostly facial expression and movement, more positive responses

Style of adult: evenly distributed between verbal and movement with a limited number of positive responses

Interactive responses are recorded only if sequence indicates that there is response to the communication in either direction (child to adult or adult to child).

*Interactive Responses for Each Dyad*

> Carol and Billy Sequence 1
> 4 verbal interactions
> 3 facial interactions
> 0 movement interaction
>
> Carol and Billy Sequence 2
> 3 verbal interactions
> 2 facial interactions
> 2 movement interactions
>
> Barbara and Thomas
> 3 verbal interactions
> 1 facial interaction
> 1 movement interaction
>
> Peg and Alfred
> 3 verbal interactions
> 1 facial interaction
> 1 movement interaction
>
> Joan and Tony
> 1 verbal interaction
> 0 facial interaction
> 2 movement interactions

## DISCUSSION

In this preliminary pilot study, the results tend to support the hypothesis that selected behaviors in the interaction as planned and deliberately carried out by the tutor are critical to the development of a "treatment alliance." It would appear that a treatment alliance allows the tutor and child to discover together the nuances of their reciprocal exchanges and to communicate them to each other in both verbal and nonverbal behavior. Where much learning and growth had taken place, the tutor-child interactive system was facilitated by mutual responsivity and continuous modification of responses. Such a treatment alliance seemed to be associated with the a priori determination of the learning and growth of both members of the dyad.

Some problems persisted. They related primarily to the assessment of the trait characteristics of the tutor and child and its relationship to the interactive quality of the communication. The criteria for pairing, as measured by the trait scales of tutors and children, did not seem to be associated with the number of interactive responses and the progress of the dyad. In fact, one of the dyads that made the most progress had the least pairing criteria. This raised questions as to the validity of the items on the scales of traits and/or the hypothesis that this pairing is critical to the formulation of the treatment alliance. It is also possible that even when the pairing is a good one, there are other more significant factors to be considered. For example, the amount of progress may be more related to the degree of authoritarianism versus permissiveness, flexibility versus rigidity on the part of the tutor and even, possibly, ethnic and other cultural considerations.

One unanticipated bonus of the project was that it was possible to analyze the reciprocal communication system. By separating the variables in the communication system into movement, facial expression, and verbalization, the individual's primary mode of communication became evident. This could be an important piece of information in the understanding of the treatment process and, in fact, may be more of a key to a match that might correlate with learning and growth. For example, in the case of Carol and Billy (where the progress was excellent), the communication systems of both tended to emphasize verbal reinforcement. In the case of Barbara and Thomas, again with excellent learning and growth, the communication system tended to be more positive facial expression and movement, with a moderate amount of verbalization. This finding was surprising because Barbara was highly intellectual and Thomas was a very verbal child. In the case of Joan and Tony, where little progress took place, Joan's communication tended to be both verbal and movement, whereas Tony's was more facial and movement. In the case of Peg and Alfred, where learning and growth was moderate, Peg's communication system was mostly verbal whereas the child's was mostly movement with some facial expression. Further investigation of the mode of the communication and the importance of a match in this area needs to be examined. It may be that the similarity hypothesis (Pulakos & Wexley, 1983) is more pertinent than the pairing notion.

It is apparent that this is just a preliminary study and one cannot generalize from so few cases. However, it highlights the need for further research of the interactive process between adults and children and suggests that there may be some meaningful reciprocal influences that affect cognitive learning and growth. It might prove helpful to set criteria for interaction as follows:

    0 to 35% interaction ............poor interaction
    35 to 65% interaction ............average interaction
    65 to 99% interaction ............excellent interaction

Another and perhaps more significant way to categorize the data might be in the actual number of interactive positive responses. The number of interactive responses recorded ranged from 2.5 to 9.3. Categories might therefore be established as follows:

    0 to 3 responses .................poor interactive communication
    4 to 7 responses .................fair interactive communication
    8 and above responses ...........excellent interactive
                                      communication

The planning of remedial strategies based on the child's mode of communication would be another area of possible research, in which the child could be grouped and taught by his or her primary mode of communication.

CHAPTER **8**

# Case Study I:
# A Feisty Boy

RUTH/STEVEN DYAD

*Graduate-Student Tutor: Ruth*

Ruth was a matriculated student at Bank Street College of Education in the Special Education Program. She was 32 years old when she entered the Learning Lab Program.

She had worked as a co-teacher in a federally funded program, integrating language-delayed preschoolers and kindergarten-age children into regular classrooms. She designed a program and taught in a basic skills program for retarded adults and did an internship developing a language stimulation program at a training school for re-

---

Much of this case study was prepared by the supervisor and graduate-student tutor.

131

tarded children in Colorado. She did her field work with normal nine- and ten-year-olds, and later with neurologically impaired children.

Her supervisor wrote the following about Ruth in her year-end case study:

> Ruth is a solid individual. Her disposition is generally radiant. She's in touch with her feelings and has a good sense of herself. She can be touched by people, but can assess people and situations. She also has a good sense of humor, a very good sense of values and is almost—is, in fact—crusader for what she thinks is right.
>
> She is resilient and has the ability to cope with frustrations; to pick up cues verbally and nonverbally; to use her past experience to synthesize and to apply theoretical knowledge to practical situations. Ruth is not threatened by criticism, and has the ability to separate her personal feelings from work situations.

## Type of Child Desired

Ruth asked for a "feisty boy," one who would fight back. She preferred a young boy between seven and nine years of age with academic problems, especially in reading. She likes kids with negative responses.

## The Child: Steven

Steven is an attractive, well-put-together eight-year-old boy. He is lean, with good muscle tone and coordination in walking and running. He seems shy and deals with his anxiety in a joking, tough guy manner. He appears adequately nourished and cared for in his dress and grooming. His parents are divorced; he lives with his mother who works, and he has a dog and a cat. He has no siblings and sees his father rarely. He was referred because he read two years below grade level.

## Family Background

Steven's father walked out on mother, thus creating havoc in the home. Mother tends to be a dependent, nervous woman, who was completely unprepared for this crisis and has difficulty organizing her life without her husband. She has been unable to cope with this boy's manipulative and negative behavior.

## Screening

A brief description based on observations of Steven by Learning Lab staff in the school setting was developed along the following screening dimensions:

Steven—eight-year-old boy
*Physical:* Small, pencil in mouth, slow to perform.
*Affect:* Little eye contact, poor self-image, immature, shy, infantile with peers, clowns.
*Temperament:* Fidgety, distractible, unable to focus, impulsive, active.
*Perceptual-Motor:* Spatial orientation confusion, right hand—tight grip.
*Cognition:* Normal IQ, logical and good concepts, good vocabulary and content, infantile tone.
*Skills:* Reading—weakness; Spelling—weakness; Writing—writes poorly, capital letters mixed with part lower case.

These observations and comments were supplemented by Steven's parents' comments and the comments of a school psychologist administering a test battery. His mother described him as "witty, high strung, nervous, strong-willed, hard to control, lacking self-confidence, and tending to give up." The psychologist described him as "negative, angry, having low frustration tolerance and poor controls, impulsive, and restless." His teacher said he was "disruptive and insulted others, lacked confidence and had large mood swings." She also observed that all his basic skills were delayed.

## The Pairing

Steven and Ruth were paired by the director of the Learning Lab on the basis of several kinds of information and insight into both Steven and Ruth, as well as on principles of teacher-child matching.

Ruth described herself in her paper on psychosocial influences:

I am the second of four children, born to parents who very much wanted each of us and loved and cared for us equally. . . . We were responsible for monitoring ourselves and trusted to make decisions concerning our lives. They [parents] were there as a resource and always available to us. . . . One expression of feeling was not modeled for us—anger. . . . I rarely heard shouting, angry voices, or saw ways of expressing anger. . . . Consequently, both my parents had ulcers and the four of us have had to explore anger as adults.

Ruth continues:

I developed normally until I went to school. . . . I had difficulty learning to read. . . . I retained my feelings of being competent but sustained them through my family rather than school. . . . My feelings of competence, independence, and discipline all combine into an intact, healthy, self-concept.

In addition to Ruth's personal essay, Ruth was asked to briefly indicate the kind of child she would like to work with. She specified the following type of child: a learning-disabled boy, seven to nine years of age—a boy, because, as she said, "Boys are tough, harder to work with, and in the classroom they are more difficult."

A decision was made that Ruth, a healthy, intact personality who had experienced feelings of negativism about learning to read in school should be offered a choice from among children who had combinations of the following characteristics:

1) Reading problem
2) Preferably a male between seven and nine
3) Experiencing negative feelings about self
4) Active and denying
5) Average intelligence
6) Poor controls

The reason for the above is as follows: A child with poor controls, need for clowning, and negative feelings about himself needs a tutor who has a strong intact personality, one who has shared some of the same negative experiences but overcome them, and one who is well organized, calm, structured and conveys a sense of firmness and order. All this adds up to Ruth.

Ruth looked at several boys before making her choice. She liked Steven's manner, described by her supervisor as the "gets-away-from-me tough guy." He was aware he was being looked at and she liked the idea that he was feisty enough to say, "Back off." In the final matching decision Ruth got the type of child she specified.

## The Tutorials

The tutorials began during the last week of November. According to Ruth's log, she picked Steven up at his school at 9:00 A.M. and rode with him on the bus to Bank Street College where they worked together in an office for approximately one hour, which included five to ten minutes for socializing around the snack table with other tutors and children in the Learning Lab practicum. Steven was picked up at Bank Street at 10:30 A.M. by an adult assigned to return him to school.

Ruth made the following observations concerning the early tutorial sessions in her Six-Week Summary: Steven seemed hesitant, lacking in confidence and angry, as a function of his inability to perform well in school. He was functioning below grade level in all academic areas. Ruth found him well motivated, competitive and developmentally on target—"forming a positive sense of industry." It was hard for him to form a relationship with her but progress was being made. Ruth described Steven as controlled, cautious, quiet, and well behaved in the one-to-one situation.

She observed that in contrast with Steven's good gross-motor coordination he had "inconsistent" fine motor control. Specifically, Ruth observed that he often lost the order in sequential tasks, such as dealing cards, counting, sorting, and rhythmic activities using his hands and feet. She requested an evaluation by the pediatrician who was part of the interdisciplinary team. The pediatric report is as follows:

He handles his anxiety in a joking manner. His attentional mechanism seems adequate but he has some tendency to be impulsive.

*Lateral Preference*
Left-handed, right-eyed, mixed foot
*Gross Motor*
Good
*Fine Motor Coordination*
Quite a bit of overflow activity (which is usually gone by six years of age). He has sequencing errors and can't keep up a pattern of alternating movements. He exhibits dyskinesis (spread of muscle activity), also mirror movements and posturing and dysrhythmia (failure to keep a regular beat, especially in the feet). He definitely has a fine motor developmental delay.
*Memory*
He has some difficulty in memory, i.e., a problem learning sequences such as the days of the week, months of the year, etc. Not a short-term auditory memory because his sentence recall is at an 11-year-old level and his digit span recall is at a 10-year-old level. Backwards, he makes consistent reversals and can't do it on a five-year-old level, which reflects a problem of sequencing information.
*Language*
My hunch is that receptive language is in the superior range, expressive language is good if he doesn't have to be specific; significant word-finding problems. It is useful to look at his style when naming the pictures. He uses associate paraphrases, his concepts are good, and he doesn't quite get the correct word. His raw score is within the norm but the difference between his receptive and expressive language is a weakness for him. He has some degree of problem learning symbolic material in sequences, rapid recall, and expressive language.

## The Tutor's Teaching Strategies

Ruth stated, as her current and ongoing goals for her work with Steven, the development of a trusting relationship and the introduction of books and beginning work on his reading skills. These goals were translated into plans for and assessments of each tutorial session. An example of Steven's writing gives some indication of his level of functioning (Figure 1).

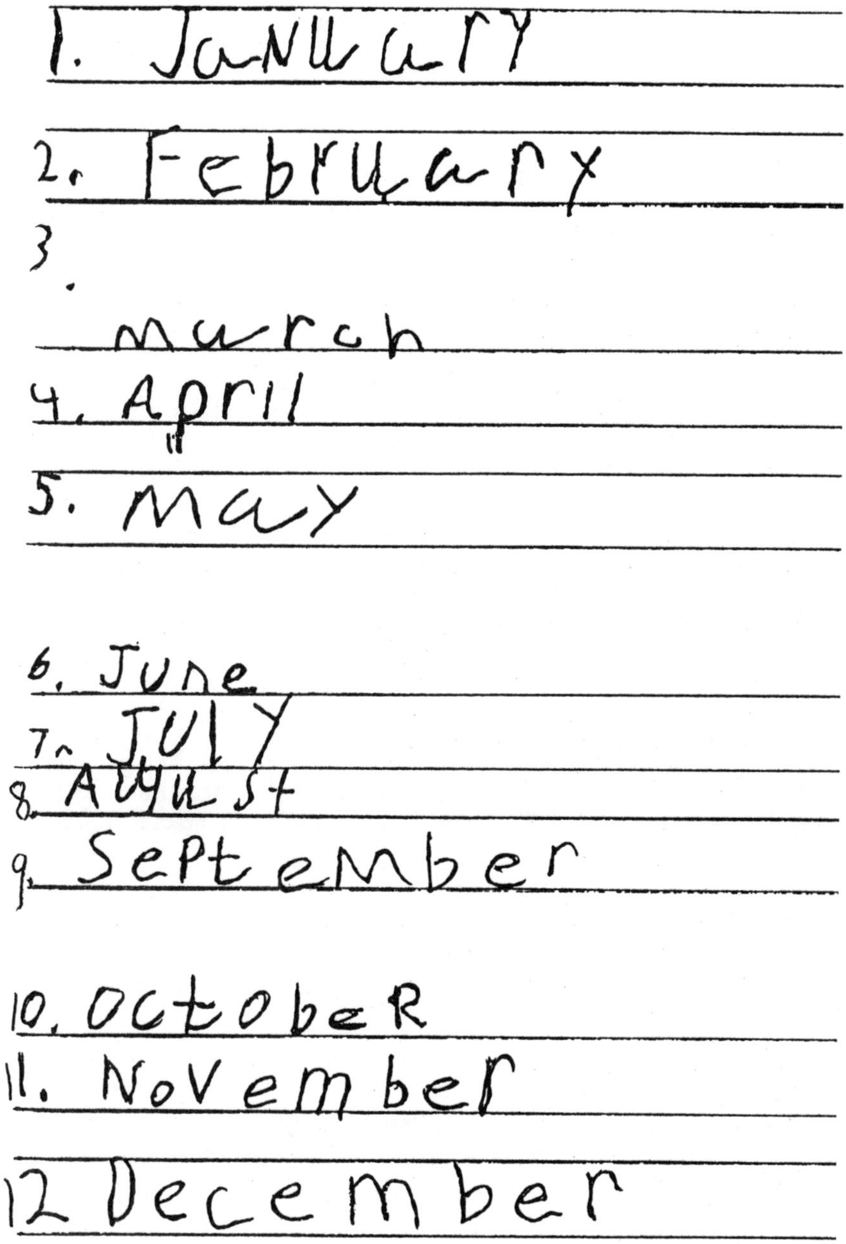

1. January

2. February

3.

   march

4. April

5. May

6. June

7. July

8. August

9. September

10. October

11. November

12. December

Figure 1

Some of the strategies adopted at this point are summarized by R. as follows:

> We used DLM-structured writing paper to improve letter formations, spatial organization, and use of upper and lower case letters. I recognized that writing was difficult for him and that it wasn't totally under his control, and commented on his good use of compensatory techniques. He decided he would make an extra effort to be neat and to turn the paper when he draws to get better control.
>
> Steven remained guarded and avoided any reading for four months, in which time a bond was established that finally permitted him to expose himself and read. He consented to appear on videotape, at which time he read two riddle books but physically tried to control the situation. It was at this time that I was able to talk to him about the things he does well and the things that give him difficulty. He began to display his humor and sense of teasing. He seemed to have freed energy that was formerly tied up in defending himself and avoiding situations. He was less angry and anxious and when these behaviors did appear they were easily traceable to a specific incident and could be channeled. We had made a connection and a commitment to each other. His commitment was to attempt risky situations and mine was to support his efforts so as to minimize the risk of failure.
>
> Steven responds best to structure, a direct verbal approach, a sharing of control and consistency. He doesn't like to feel pressured or rushed into a situation; he needs extra time to get acclimated. He is a strong child and counts on strength and guidance from adults.

By April, Ruth had a more precise understanding of Steven's strengths and weaknesses. In her later summary she could break down his performance and behavior into a table of strengths and weaknesses as can be seen on page 139.

Ruth said of Steven that his anxiety was so great that it always sabotaged his performance, and the cycle of failure-anxiety-failure was disastrous. She found he had an unusually great need for control and that this emerged in his social relationships where he had adopted the strategy of using inanimate objects to make contact. In particular he had a ventriloquist act that permitted him to express his feeling quite freely. The Draw-A-Person (Figure 2) illustrates this—it is a picture

| Dimension | Strengths | Weaknesses |
|---|---|---|
| Temperament | good attentional mechanism, not distractible | slow to warm up, impulsive |
| Affect | imaginative, joking | anxious, angry, negative |
| Perceptual-Motor | good auditory and visual, good gross motor skills | fine motor delay which affects writing, drawing |
| Language | good expressive and receptive language | difficulty organizing tasks |
| Social Behavior and Responses | joking, a performer | appears indifferent, insecure |
| Basic Skills | good sight and phonics math—poor | poor spelling, doesn't apply knowledge, writing is poor |

of Charlie McCarthy. She found that his intelligence and superior language ability caused pain by making him extremely aware of his failure in other areas. Ruth said of his skills that writing was a difficult task for him—he mixed upper and lower case letters and his placement and spacing were poor:

> In April he was able to read all the words on the Dolch list through third grade. He read the Harris Oral Paragraphs A and B with no errors and good comprehension, but would not even begin on Section C. When I read it orally, he could answer all the questions.
> In Math, he is able to count orally to 100 correctly; can count by two's to 100 using pennies; attends to only one attribute at a time; has difficulty continuing an established pattern of more than two things. Can do one place addition and subtraction in his head, can do two place operations on paper. Doesn't understand place value, especially evident when using nickles and dimes.

Ruth's goals for Steven as of mid-April were to continue working on sequential tasks; do games using words with medial vowels; read about baseball; assist in organizing tasks; continue to provide a sheltered environment to express his feelings and "risk" difficult situations.

Figure 2

## Small Group Meetings with Supervisor

Ruth's supervisory group consisted of a supervisor and three other graduate students. The group met for one hour after tutorial sessions ended.

The agenda for the small group called for each graduate student to report on the work with her child, focusing on what she had learned about the child. Often, the children were discussed in terms of required readings. The videotapes of tutor-child interactions were viewed and discussed in these meetings. Preparations were made for sharing these tapes with the interdisciplinary team in the seminar.

The graduate students became more open with each other as they began to discuss their work with the children and the amount of sharing and supportiveness increased. At first Ruth was restrained with her suggestions to others. She later became a consistently sharing person—serious, yet understanding.

The group meeting was always followed by individual conferences with the supervisor, in which there was less discussion of the "whys" and "whats" and more of the "hows."

## Seminars

Videotapes were made periodically of Ruth and Steven's interactions and were reviewed by the interdisciplinary team in seminar sessions. Following is an excerpt from one seminar. All students, the entire staff, Steven's school teacher, and his former reading teacher were present.

*Tutor:* Steven is eight years, 10 months, in Mrs. T's 3-4 class. He has some really good skills as far as phonics and sight vocabulary. He has some difficulty with fine motor functioning. The pediatrician did a workup and found that he had fine motor development delay which influences his writing and his ability to sequence tasks. We've been working on sequencing, time, the days and months, things like that.

*Teacher:* His background knowledge is a lot more than he can verbalize. When you get into a conversation with him, it's amazing the kind of things that come out. He's scientifically oriented. He has a lot of information on animals. He's very interested in space—he's seen "Star Wars" about six times. He's made a lot of puppets. He's extremely artistic. He's made puppets of the characters in "Star Wars," and he knows their names, what they said. All these puppets are very artistically done. It amazes me. Yet when it comes to academic work, reading and writing, there's a tremendous discrepancy.

## Videotape Shown to Interdisciplinary Team

*Director:* Look at the way this child defends himself . . . we're laughing . . . he's making all those faces the whole time . . . here's the drawing . . . he starts with the shoulders, then he does the feet . . . then he turns it and does the next part . . . everything is built from the bottom upwards . . . he does not put the head on . . . it tells us about the motor problem, how he feels about it, how he defends himself . . . he's defending himself against any possible reading.
*Student:* Do all his drawings get done that way?
*Psychologist:* He's turning the paper. . . .
*Director:* A good example of *excellent compensation* . . . what is he conveying to me? Right, that he's in control of me. Complete resistance . . . he did all that detail and still there's no head on his drawing. No hands . . . he was making a dummy, a ventriloquist's dummy . . . he relates in this way. What does that mean?
*Student:* It means that he feels himself out of control. Somebody else has control. . . .
*Director:* He has need to communicate through a third person. He feels he can't control himself. It has two implications: that he cannot do it because of lack of control, and that he might also get punished. Also, he can get recognition this way without being accountable for anything he does. It's a very important message. It allows him to be negative, angry, anything he wants to be. You're dealing with a very bright kid, a very defended child, and one who can really manage his life—unsuccessfully. . . . More about the picture . . . the dummy has no hands. It prevents him from feeling aggressive . . . he would like to strike out. He has found this way to allow himself to control his feelings and manage to express them nevertheless. This is tremendously valuable for this child, and I wouldn't take it away for many reasons. On the other hand, until he can work through and get it out in the open, nothing much is going to happen. Here you have a child with fine motor deficiency but also it gives you an

example of a child who wil not take the chance. An example of a primary emotional problem. . . . Let's see how he reads. . . .

Ruth found the viewing of tapes in seminar a valuable experience. She always rose to the occasion, pulling out the salient features of her work with Steven and developing a constructive presentation. It demanded that she be clear and precise, and she felt it helped prepare her for interdisciplinary situations. She liked getting feedback from everyone.

## Counseling Steven's Mother

Steven's mother was a faithful participant in our parent group and individual meetings. She spoke freely of her problems with Steven, many of which were centered on his uncontrollable and negative behavior. She, herself, had not resolved problems resulting from the separation from her husband. She shared her feelings of helplessness, depression, and vulnerability. Her high anxiety gave her a frenetic quality.

Steven's mother sought us out on many occasions to discuss her many concerns about herself and her child and to role-play ways she could help Steven gain some confidence and control. Slowly she was able to make changes in her attitude and style with the child. She obtained a job and began to experience lessening of anxiety. More of her energy was freed to help the child, reorganize her life, and develop some consistent patterns at home.

During May and June, individual conferences centered on future plans for mother and child. Opportunities became available for Steven's mother to work and live upstate (where her family lived) so that she could avail herself of family supports. This was encouraged, after much discussion, because a major problem had been her alienation from family and friends and her inability to admit the failure of her marriage.

Presented here is an excerpt of a parent meeting toward the end of the year. The tutor, supervisor, parent counselor and Steven's mother were present.

*Mother:* Steven has, I think, some conceptual gaps. Things that I would have thought he would have mastered, he hasn't. They are curious things . . . I just kept getting the feeling that he wasn't ready for some of the experiences when we had them. . . . It's hard to go back and give him these things. They are hard to uncover. They come up in funny ways.

He did have a period in his younger life when it was chaotic for both of us, and that may have caused a lot of these kinds of things. There was a period in our life when I didn't know if I was coming or going, and I'm sure he didn't either.

*Tutor:* That might be a piece of it. . . . The pediatrician looked at Steven and found that he had a fine motor developmental delay. It wasn't anything very big, but just for his age level he was a little bit behind. To me that says something about the readiness of his system. Maybe three or four years ago—he was probably a little behind at that point—things that he should have been gleaning, he wasn't. And if the environment was a little chaotic, I think that may have compounded it, but part of it is within him.

*Mother:* That's interesting. I never noticed it.

*Tutor:* Like his writing. . . .

*Mother:* I know his writing, but I always thought that was because he didn't want to write.

*Tutor:* No, part of it is that it is really hard for him . . . even when he really tries he can't seem to do it . . . in his drawing, he turns the paper. He has found lots of ways to compensate. I asked him about that yesterday. He was drawing me some pictures: "Steven, do you know why you turn the paper?" And he said, "So I can see better." His perception of why he does it is interesting. When he is highly motivated, as when he draws, he can find that extra ounce of carefulness.

*Mother:* I never would have thought of that.

*Counselor:* I don't think it's anything unusual. It's a discrepancy within him.

*Mother:* But it's something that he will eventually overcome?

*Supervisor:* It's just developmental. His body is moving at it's own pace. I think with a boy and a boy like Steven, mothers tend to say, "Well, it's all emotional."

*Mother:* I did! A lot of things that I expected from S. at his age—I wondered, thinking back . . . I don't say anything to Steven, because I don't like to make him feel any stigma . . . I notice things sometimes, like I tried to get him to help me with the dishes recently. He hates to do it, but I feel like it's good practice for him. I watch him, and it really is such a struggle, but I feel like it's a good experience for him . . . to do that, to train himself.

*Tutor:* With practice he gets a little better. There's no question about that.

### Summary of Child's Progress (From Ruth's Case Study)

Steven has made subtle, yet vital changes during our time together. Since he has risked reading and discovered what a capable reader he is, his anger and anxiety have lessened. He has an active imagination that he utilizes in the development of skits he writes for his ventriloquist dummy and puppets. His use of fantasy to vent his frustrations, and to cope with anxiety-producing situations in a creative, constructive way, indicates his ego strength. He is able to apply his creative intelligence to achieve a long-range goal through mastery and competence, which is supporting his self-image. He is less dependent on academic success to validate his self-worth, so he is more available to learning and can take risks academically.

Temperamentally he is always going to be slow to warm up, but his impulsivity and initial negativism lessened as I began allowing extra time in transitions and had written agendas so that his indifferent listening didn't deprive him of the information needed. His affect and social behavior also illustrate the change. He is less anxious and angry; he appears more able to cope with his frustrations and ventilate them through appropriate channels, rather than kicking doors, snapping at people, and being resistant. The videotapes reinforce these observations. In December he was resistant to go on tape. Once he agreed, he needed to keep control of the situation and never established eye contact. The second time, he read for the first time with me, still anxious but better able to cope. The third time, he put on a performance with his puppets and was able to express how nervous he was. He has grown!

Ruth's supervisor wrote the following concerning Steven's growth:

With each new or uncovered asset, his self-concept has improved. His well of ego strength has indicated to us that he can function, that he can accept and respond to verbal and nonverbal cues, that his responses are reality-based in that he is not impulse-ridden and can control his impulsivity. He is now successful with certain tasks including reading. To sum up, his deficits are based on a specific learning disability and not on a deficit of ego strength.

Steven's progress, as evidenced by formal testing, is shown below. The test scores and language profiles illustrate progress in all areas. The largest gains are in reading, language, and self-concept. These were the major goals of the educational therapy.

Following are the results of the test battery administered at the beginning of the year (pre) and at the end (post), and, on page 147, a profile of the language pre and post.

| Test Data | Pre | Post |
|---|---|---|
| DAPT | 29 | 88 |
| Bender-Gestalt (score) | 7 (error score) | 6 (error) |
| WRAT: Reading | 2.3 (grade) | 5.1 (grade) |
|       Spelling | 2.0 (grade) | 2.9 (grade) |
|       Arithmetic | 2.8 (grade) | 3.0 (grade) |
| Picture Completion of WISC | 14 | 18 |

| Language Sample | Pre | Post |
|---|---|---|
| Function | 3 | 5 |
| Syntax | 3 | 5 |
| Cognitive Style | 4 | 4 |
| Expressive Style | 3 | 6 |
| WISC Vocabulary | 9 | 9 |
| WISC Block Design | 8 | 8 |
| Peabody Age | 7/10 age | 8/5 age |
| Gray Oral Reading Paragraphs Administered: | not scorable | 4.4 grade |

Below is an excerpt from Steven's mother's Parent Questionnaire concerning how she perceived the year to have gone.

Q. What changes have you noticed this year?
A. Wonderful changes. His attitudes towards new experiences, more willing. In behavior with others, he gets along well with other kids, more friends, more self-confident, more

## Language Profile

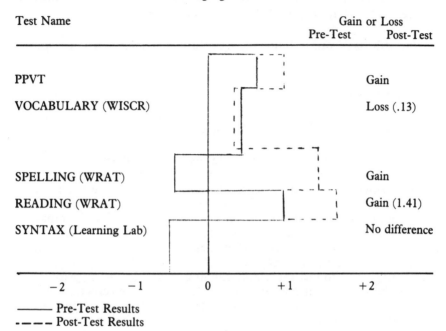

| Test Name | Gain or Loss |
| --- | --- |
| | Pre-Test        Post-Test |
| PPVT | Gain |
| VOCABULARY (WISCR) | Loss (.13) |
| SPELLING (WRAT) | Gain |
| READING (WRAT) | Gain (1.41) |
| SYNTAX (Learning Lab) | No difference |

——— Pre-Test Results
– – – Post-Test Results

mature, less babyish, doesn't act like a child when things
don't go well.
Q. Does your child work better, have more friends or feel better
about himself? Is he *easier to get along with* and more helpful?
A. Yes.
Q. Was this contact helpful?
A. This place has helped me to help him, i.e., with the dummy
he made he wouldn't have accepted help but now he can
listen (a little). Comes to me with math problems, but I'm
not good at explaining, but he's gained a great deal. Everything has been so much nicer with Steven since he's gone to
Bank Street.

At the end-of-the-year discussion with Steven's teacher, Steven's
mother commented:

Academically there's some movement. His math is OK and he
is able to ask for help. His reading is more fluid, and he seems
to get some enjoyment from it."

She believed that Bank Street had given him a chance to know himself better and feel appreciated. But, she continued:

He still has trouble following directions and needs step by step input.

### Progress of Tutor

Concerning Ruth's growth, her supervisor wrote:

I see Ruth's growth in this field (learning disabilities) directly related to the trials and tribulations in S.'s progress. Her log is a step-by-step account of that process and it could be constructively used as a reference by anyone working with a child with a configuration of problems similar to Steven's. The Thomas, Chess, and Birch book, *Temperament and Behavior Disorders in Children*, made a very important contribution to her work with Steven. In terms of herself, if you were to ask Ruth which of the readings she found most enlightening, I would be surprised if she didn't say that De Hirsch (1977) article on interaction. We read it; we discussed it. She was able to relate it in many ways to her work with Steven and to her feelings. Their reference to rescue fantasies and Selma's (the author's) tape with Steven helped her to realize that she didn't have to protect Steven or worry about him anymore.

### Progress of Mother

Steven's mother, writing the following year from her new home upstate, says:

We have since moved upstate to Schenectady. If there is a school or affiliation or Bank Street here, I would really like to know. Steven is taking time in adjusting and I would like to give him help in academic areas, but as his mother, he is resistant to me.

We miss Bank Street and all the wonderful caring people there. If Steven's teacher is still there, please send our love and tell her we miss her.

*Summary of Case Study*

All aspects of the Clinical Teaching Model practiced at Bank Street's Child Service Demonstration Center are presented in this case study.

Fundamental changes in the total functioning of the child—social, emotional, cognitive and academic—are evident in the interviews with mother, tutor, supervisor, and teacher. The post-test battery confirms the qualitative data.

This case is a good illustration of the significance of the pairing between tutor and child. This suitable match allows, encourages, and enhances the growth of both the child and graduate student as they mesh together in a learning, supportive, growth environment.

# CHAPTER 9

# Case Study II:
# A Bright Worrier

---

## JANE/DAVID DYAD

*Graduate-Student Tutor: Jane*

Jane, David's tutor, is a woman in her early forties who is married and has two college-age children. She has been teaching for 11 years in kindergarten, second, and now third grade. She has a B.A. from Vassar in History, an M.S. from Bank Street in Early Childhood, and is currently working on a Professional Diploma in order to be a reading specialist.

Initial impressions are of a quiet and reserved, yet warm and likable woman, and an experienced, sensitive teacher. She appears to have

---

Much of this case study was prepared by the supervisor and graduate-student tutor.

a well-balanced perspective on situations, is considerate, and has a strong sense of self.

## Type of Child Desired

Jane requested a young dyslexic child, quiet and on the passive side, so that she could concentrate on teaching beginning reading.

## The Child: David

David, age seven, is an observant, serious, reflective child with lovely dark eyes and a small-boned frame of below average height. He is a healthy child, though a poor eater. He is ambidexterous and, according to the school, has a tendency to fall frequently. He has had two falls which have resulted in gashes requiring stitches.

## The Pairing

Jane's supervisor described how Jane and David were paired in her case summary on Jane, as follows:

> She wanted to work with a boy with beginning reading difficulties in second or third grade because she had taught girls of his age. She was eager for a change, yet wanted an age group she felt competent teaching.
>
> After observing several children in the local public school, she did not feel that she "knew any of them well enough" to make a decision. She consulted with the Learning Lab director, who felt David needed the most help; Jane took him eagerly on this advice. Later, the teacher expressed satisfaction with this choice, as she described David as "a bundle of nerves" and too passive to succeed without specific outside help. David was a virtual non-reader early in the year.

The Learning Lab director had observed David in his classroom before three choices were given to each graduate student. She made careful note of this boy's awareness of his difficulty. He had a second-grade workbook open on his desk and was busily writing in the workbook. As the director moved about the room, it was evident that David just made any marks in his workbook, attempting to make it look as though he was competent and able to deal with the material. When asked, he did not want anyone to see or know his failure. Only when he was out of the reach of his teacher and classroom buddies did he confide that he could not read and did not understand what was expected of him. In talking with David it became evident that this was a very bright dyslexic child, with high level conceptual ability covering up his inadequacies.

The match of David and Jane was made because Jane was also a bright intellectual who had a commitment to learning and teaching. Her successful experiences were primarily with such bright, middle-class children. She was clear, structured, and cognitively well organized—just what the Learning Lab director felt was lacking in his teacher and at home.

## The Tutorials

David's tutor was sensitive to David's interests and she seemed to understand his strengths and weaknesses. The early programs Jane planned for David demonstrated her ability to work with all aspects of his personal makeup. Jane's supervisor's summary of Jane's early work with David gives a clear picture of how he functioned at the beginning of his participation in the Learning Lab:

"She was sensitive to him as a whole child—not just his weaknesses, but his strengths as well. She recorded his interests in sports, space, drawing, monkeys, dinosaurs, and monsters. She was aware of his anxiety but also of his curiosity, humor, and playfulness. She saw his temperament as persistent and reflective. His good language, wealth of information, and logical, well-organized thinking all reflected his strong intellect. She was concerned about his shyness socially and his poor reading skills."

Throughout November, December, and early January, his skills were assessed and different approaches were tried with him. Jane felt David's visual perception of words to be somewhat unstable and his visual memory weak. He sometimes had difficulty with visual sequencing of letters in words. He had some sight words but did not appear to know any phonics beyond initial consonant sounds and some blends. David's comprehension was good. He often predicted and extended ideas and concepts of what he was reading.

Jane's supervisor was particularly satisfied with Jane's choice of teaching strategies for David through the course of the year. In her summary of the year's tutorials, Jane's supervisor described Jane's initial goals in her work with David and the means whereby she successfully achieved them. The full range of activities which Jane and David pursued together are described in the following excerpt from the case summary.

Jane stated in November that she wanted "to find a way into reading that worked for David and help him become aware of his own strengths and strategies so that he could begin to help himself, and also to help him relax so that he could put his energy into learning and regain his confidence through success.

The way in which Jane achieved these goals reflects the attributes that she brought to the task. She had a natural enjoyment of all people, which was clearly evident in her interaction with David. She chose activities that wouldn't threaten him academically, yet would provide him with specific focus. After the first two sessions she recorded her observations of him, including a detailed section about how "his good self-conduct is undermined by his worrying about his abilities, which blocks him from doing what he can do." She also listed his strengths and weaknesses, several questions she would like to address in her next session, and three approaches to take with David, one of which was to "share with him his strengths so he can be conscious of using them." She felt that she couldn't have had a better match.

Her organization and planning were always connected with her reflections on her work with David. She was insightful into his affect and tried to address his needs through the academics, yet she never ignored his anxiety.

She provided support and an opportunity to succeed by assigning him reading tasks he could do, i.e., using picture cues, reading his own experience stories, and gradually building up a sight vocabulary. She acknowledged his interests and strengths in order to help lessen his anxiety which she thought sabotaged his performance. She encouraged him to draw pictures of things that were important to him and dictate stories about them, which they then compiled into a book. Role-playing and reading games with puppets he had made were relaxing activities they enjoyed together.

Her genuine interest in and appreciation of David were conveyed to him through her choice of activities; also through the respect she gave him while he talked, worked, and traveled to

Bank Street. She allowed him the opportunity to move at his own pace, yet provided structure, organization, and a challenge that supported and motivated him.

She prepared him for transitions in activities, gave him choices, switched from tedious skill tasks to more engaging activities, permeated with a sense of calm that was impressive. She was direct with David and asked him what he would like to learn. She shared her reasons for doing tasks that he would rather have avoided.

Jane's ability to achieve such a strong treatment alliance with David was impressive. Jane's personal qualities which made this relationship possible are described below.

She is genuinely warm and caring and responds to the subtle nuances that convey anxiety, fatigue, and frustration. She is supportive of a child's performance and empathetic with his struggle, not manipulated by it. Her ability to evaluate when anxiety was beneficial and when it became detrimental to performance has grown during the year. She could keep sight of a goal without allowing it to rigidly dictate the rate or direction of sessions.

She was flexible in her methods and plans in a way that included David and respected his interests and concerns. She developed materials and games based on his interests and then incorporated the specific skills that she felt he needed. When his love of and ability to illustrate stories was discovered, she extended it imaginatively. She introduced books illustrated by someone she knew and then followed it up by suggesting that David write to the illustrator. The pride he took in composing his letter, recopying it, and including an illustration of his own was only one of many high points in their relationship.

## Summary of Tutorials

David's tutorial experience had several turning points, evidenced by his growing confidence in social situations and his increasing willingness to read. David's progress and Jane's careful planning that brought about the changes are summarized below.

Jane felt that the end of January was a breakthrough point in her work with David. She suggested two factors that had a combined effect. He was promoted to a new reading group in school, and she began her second session each week with him. There was a marked change in their relationship after this. David was more open about himself and began to exhibit more of this humor. It was as though he totally trusted Jane and no longer was overly concerned about his vulnerability. She wouldn't let him fail, and he seemed to sense that.

The content of their work became focused on academics now. She used trial lessons for teaching spelling, reviewed what worked and what didn't, discovered he did best when he spelled orally rather than in writing, and pointed this out to him. She was teaching him word families, sight words, and medial vowels, using games they designed and made together.

When she finally got him to read from a book, to which he'd been resistant, she discovered strategies that helped him decode, i.e., rhyming words, using contextual clues, and looking at the configuration of the word. She then provided easy-to-read books that engaged David's imagination and humor. This provided the motivation to persevere when the reading was difficult. Throughout this period her support of him was honest and constant. Rather than letting him struggle, she would remind him of the rule he'd learned that would help him in decoding a word. She'd give the vowel sound or whatever he needed to succeed. She made copious notes of his errors. When a pattern emerged, she could teach him strategies that worked.

By mid-February David appeared more confident academically and socially. He talked more freely with adults and children, even volunteering to read books from the Monster Series to another child, while waiting in the lobby. He confided his fears and concerns to Jane about his language arts teacher at school, difficulty with class directions, and his thoughts on death. He began to make suggestions for projects they could do together and Jane listened and followed whenever possible.

By March he was still relying on context rather than phonics, as this was more natural for him. He read signs everywhere, learning to decode words at a rapid rate. He asked to take books home to read with his parents. He was eager to read independently and showed more confidence. Figure 3 is an illustration of David's handwriting. In April when Jane began to prepare for their separation, they talked about plans for the summer. David asked if she would work with him next year and was disappointed that she couldn't. He told her, "I

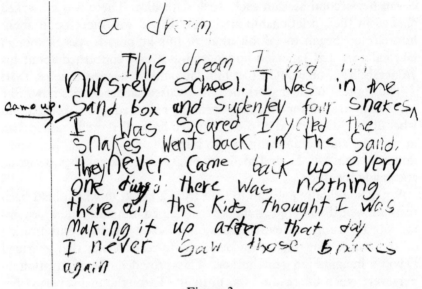

a dream,

This dream I had in
Nursrey School. I was in the
Sand box and Sudenley four snakes,
I was scared I ycled the
snakes went back in the sand,
they never came back up every
one digs' there was nothing
there all the kids thought I was
Making it up after that day
I never saw those snakes
again

came up →

Figure 3

want to work with you. I can't learn from anyone else." Then he
asked if he could have a "correspondence course over the summer."
Jane said she would write to him but she wouldn't give him work to
do.

Their tutorial sessions still included reading, a word review, usually
a game to reinforce skills, but was expanded to include dictation and
some math work. As usual, they were occupied in meaningful work.
David continued to have problems following written directions in his
classroom. Jane developed a game format in which he had to read
written directions to win. By April Jane had gained a precise understanding of David's strengths and weaknesses in terms of the seven
observational dimensions emphasized in the Practicum. They are
listed in the table on page 157.

Following is Jane's description of the direction and focus for future
sessions which accompanied the April profile of David's strengths and
weaknesses.

David's profile of strengths and weaknesses indicates a need
for concentration in certain areas. In the perceptual dimension,
his poor revisualization of words when writing them continues

| Dimension | Strengths | Weaknesses |
|---|---|---|
| Physical | | |
| Speech | clear articulation | very soft voice |
| Motor | well coordinated | falls often |
| Grapho-Motor | | loose control |
| Social | well related | reserved |
| Temperament | persistent, focused | over-cautious |
| Affect | curious, competitive | vulnerable to failure |
| Perceptual-Motor | | |
| Visual | perceives whole words | poor revisualization |
| Auditory | good discrimination of phonemes | auditory-visual integration |
| Tactile | identifies letters by touch | spatial problems |
| Cognition | | |
| Concepts | extends ideas | |
| Thought Process | analyzes easily | |
| Expressive Language | clarity of ideas expressed | written language undeveloped |
| Receptive Language | rapid comprehension | preoccupation can block reception |
| Academic Skills | | |
| Reading | comprehension | word analysis |
| Writing | legibility | letter proportion |
| Arithmetic | accuracy in computation | memory of facts |

to need attention. Using his auditory strength to compensate for the visual weakness is a good strategy. His tendency to miss details and internal letters in his first glance at words requires more focus on these elements. Further development of auditory-visual integration is also necessary so it becomes more automatic. The area requiring the most attention at the present time is writing—both in letter proportion and expression of his ideas in writing. He has neither the confidence nor skill in writing that he has achieved in reading. David's relationships with others are solid and he is self-sufficient. Because he is self-contained and reserved, I'd like to encourage him to initiate more contact with others. David's many strengths will continue to help him progress and will suggest learning strategies. Making him aware of what works for him is important.

Specifically, I plan to help his spelling by listening to, saying, blending, and writing words. Focus on phoneme patterns and grapheme-phoneme correspondence, as well as medial and final sounds, will help visual motor integration. A booklet of word families and words he can spell with sentences and pictures by him is a possible project. To motivate his writing I'd like to have him do a book about himself and illustrate it. He needs practice in writing freely, with no concern for spelling and handwriting, and also copying to focus on the latter skills. In reading, we'll continue to work on word-analysis skills and choose library books for reading at home. I'd like to explore his concepts and skills in math and check his retention of number facts.

## Graduate-Student Tutor's Assessments of David's Progress

In her year-end assessment of David's progress, Jane speaks very enthusiastically of David's achievements in reading. Jane also describes how his personal strengths have helped him to learn to compensate for his weaknesses. Prior to his participation in the Learning Lab, such problems as lack of self-confidence, high anxiety levels, and poor visual and spatial orientation seriously hindered his progress. Excerpts from Jane's summary are quoted below.

> In reviewing the steps that led to David's success in reading, I find the following things are significant. Since he had good sound discrimination and could blend, supplementary phonics work was very helpful. It gave him a system that he could use independently. His good memory for the sight words he encountered repeatedly was another strength. However, the biggest breakthrough came when David began to use his own sense of language to anticipate as he read meaningful, humorous, and interesting books of an appropriate level. Once anxiety was reduced, he was able to integrate what he knew and connect sound with symbol.
>
> In working with David, I became more sensitive to his verbal and nonverbal cues (yawning, diversionary conversation) which signaled anxiety or overloading. I could see very clearly the interaction between affect and learning—both it's positive and negative effects. His open dismay at the prospect of the termination of our work together was an unusual expression of his feelings, revealing how much he valued our time together and the support it gave him. Working with David was always a positive experience for me because he responded so well, we had good rapport, and there was a natural flow in our communication and in shifting from one activity to another.

David has progressed from a virtual non-reader to a reading level of 2.6. This progress has affected his social behavior positively, reduced his anxiety, and restored his confidence in his ability to succeed in school. I think that his intelligence, perseverance, and language strength will compensate for his visual and spatial difficulties. However, his sensitivity and need to succeed on a superior level may continue to cause some anxiety which could block learning. Another year at Bank Street would help ensure smooth progress. His teacher concurs in this recommendation because she recognizes his need for emotional support.

In May, the Pupil-Placement Test of Houghton-Mifflin was administered. David read independently on a 2.6 grade level.

*Progress of Tutor*

In assessing her growth, Jane's supervisor pointed out Jane's increased confidence in her ability to work with children with learning problems. Jane also became more sensitive to children's verbal and nonverbal cues and demonstrated her understanding of the interaction between affect and learning. She came to appreciate how important her relationship with David was to him and his academic achievements. The use of the observational dimensions as an organizing technique appealed to Jane's systematic approach to planning her program for David.

To quote Jane's supervisor, "During the year, she demonstrated her commitment to David through her contact with his teacher and her enjoyment of sharing his success with David's mother. She feels it is necessary "to have a more sympathetic view' of both parents and teachers. She is a gifted teacher who had the understanding, commitment and vitality crucial to making a significant difference in David's learning."

Jane was supportive and actively interested in the three other graduate-student tutors and their children. She offered suggestions of materials and activities as well as insights into why something did or did not work. She made statements that reflected her interest in not overshadowing or dominating the sessions. She was sensitive to others' needs. Her sense of equality was offered when she was the center of attention for too long. She was concerned about offending others and very mindful of the limited time. There is no doubt that Jane was a key contributor to the group and of great assistance to her supervisor.

*Family Background*

During that first year, David's mother had expressed her concern for David's feeling of failure in school. Her request that David be given special help brought him to the attention of the Learning Lab staff who were screening children in his school's classrooms. At the end of the first year, David had made much progress academically and some thought was given to letting him try to make it on his own. David's mother came to see the Learning Lab director to plead that David be continued for a second year. David also made a similar plea. In his own words, "I can do the work here but I still need help in school."

Unfortunately, at the beginning of David's second year with the Learning Lab, his parents separated abruptly. As a consequence of David's emotional suffering, he became depressed. He was unable to share the worries about his predicament with his tutor, but sought out the Learning Lab director with whom he had established a good bond the first year.

At first David did not speak about his family, but when he did he referred to his mother with great warmth and seemed more guarded about his father. Marital stress was reported by the school as well as talk of separation when David was younger, but this had been re-solved. David enjoys the support and companionship of his mother who reads with him regularly, an activity they both enjoy. David's nine-year-old brother had reading difficulty initially which his mother says has been overcome. David says he and his brother don't get along very well. His brother never speaks to him. His mother says that perhaps the brother is jealous of David, who is very appealing. There are grandparents in Massachusetts for whom David expresses great affection.

Figure 4 shows David's Draw-A-Person as he began in the Learning Lab. Anger seems to be the main element in a highly intellectual figure. Figure 5, drawn at the end of his second year, reveals a drawing of an active sportsman with movement and creativity and a high level of integration.

Figure 4

Figure 5

*Family Counseling*

The director first met David's mother when she was at the school. David had fallen and hurt himself and his mother was called. She appeared calm and organized and was introduced to the director of the Learning Lab. The accident was handled in a matter-of-fact way, and David's mother said she would take him to her doctor for possible stitches. The impression was that this situation might have arisen many times before.

David's mother was attractive, well spoken, and appeared to be in command. Her relationship with David seemed good and appropriate.

After David had attended Learning Lab sessions for about a month, David's mother called and said she was unable to make the group sessions and arranged for a private conference with the director and parent counselor. She revealed that her older son had also had reading problems, but as he had eventually overcome them she was not unduly alarmed. She was, however, grateful for any help she was offered and would be fully cooperative.

As the year proceeded, David made much progress; thought was given to the termination of work with David for the following year. A conference was held with David's mother and she literally begged the director and parent counselor to continue with David for the following reasons: 1) He needed the security of a one-to-one tutor for another year; 2) there were difficulties in the family situation; and 3) he requested to be continued. It was then agreed to continue with David.

As it happened, it was most important to David that the decision was made to continue. Over the summer, problems between David's mother and father became heightened. It was said by the school that the father had physically and mentally abused the mother and she had moved out of the apartment with her two children. David's depressed state became evident and the parent counselor immediately became involved with David's mother as the psychologist took on the role of therapist for David. The mother was faced with severe financial burdens, got a job, and tried to find a suitable apartment. There were many temporary moves, all of which required David to travel alone to and from school. On many occasions he went from school to his father's apartment. He was alone most of the time. His brother sometimes traveled with him but never a word passed between them. If they spent the after-school hours at their father's house, they had to travel home on public transportation at night. David described his eating habits as "too scared to eat breakfast" and helping himself to "whatever was about at night." As David began to reveal his fears to the psychologist, these were conveyed to the mother by the parent counselor. For example, David was worried about his mother, afraid something would happen to her as she had no money and only a temporary job. The mother was given practical ways to reassure David that she was allright, and that there was money for food and lodging.

Gradually, through the year, conditions got better. The family found a permanent living space, mother settled into a permanent position she liked, the children began to visit father regularly, and life became less chaotic. David's tutor helped a great deal by spending one afternoon a week at his apartment. This also enabled the tutor to make good contact with the mother and give her some needed support in her role with the children. David's mother gradually began to gain more confidence in her new role and this was reflected in the attention she was now able to provide David.

David gradually bounced back to normal and his academic work took on new meaning for him.

### Second Graduate-Student Tutor's Assessment of David's Progress

With David experiencing great distress over his parents' separation and his relocation to another apartment with his mother and brother, David made a very slow start with his second year's tutor.

David's new tutor spent the early weeks trying to establish rapport with him. She encouraged David to engage in specially chosen activities which she believed (based on Jane's reports) enjoyed. In her year-end case summary, this tutor expressed satisfaction with the gains David made from their work together. She suggested that in order to maintain these gains, David should continue to experience academic success and should achieve recognition from his classmates for his progress.

An excerpt from this second-year tutor's summary is quoted below.

His confidence rose, endurance increased, and he began reading for pleasure at a level that exceeded his school grade. Written compositions grew longer and more complex, as well as more explicit. Reading aloud, putting oral narratives of personal experience into writing (and, later, typed form) seem to have worked for David. I served as a model in both activities, emphasizing flow and spontaneity of expression rather than correctness or neatness. Processing workbook instructions and spelling both remain weak. David also needs help in learning to work more independently. The gains made this year should be maintained providing he has opportunities for further success and for recognition from classmates and teachers. His idea for a class newspaper—an outgrowth of the book developed in the Learning Lab—is an example of his ability to find effective ways of meeting his own deepest needs.

The table on page 165 shows the scores David obtained on the battery of standardized and non-standardized tests administered on four different testing occasions over a one-and-a-half year time period.

The progress in academic skills is spectacular. In third grade, David now scores at sixth-grade reading level. The high cognitive ability, combined with the supportive adult in a good treatment alliance, provides the opportunities for excellent academic achievement.

## Summary of Case Study

David's progress was confirmed by standardized and informal tests, by his tutors' remarks, and by the information obtained from his teachers and mother.

His mother stated at the end of the first year,

David's experience at Bank Street has done wonders for not only his reading skills but also his self-confidence. He's no longer afraid to try but plunges in with his new-found feeling that he can do the work. It has been a very positive experience for him and has made his life at school much happier as a consequence.

His mother stated at the end of the second year,

Self-confidence is most important. The caring quality of the people at Bank Street has been the most important. His tutor has finally become his friend. The moment I walk into Bank

| Tests | Testing Occasions | | | |
|---|---|---|---|---|
| | (1) | (2) | (3) | (4) |
| Standardized: | | | | |
| 1) Draw-a-Person Test— | | | | |
|     Standardized Score | 105 | 105 | 119 | 108 |
|     Percentile Score | 63 | 63 | 90 | 71 |
| 2) Visual Motor Gestalt Test | | | | |
|     Error Score | 2 | 5 | 2 | 2 |
| 3) WISC-R | | | | |
|     Vocabulary—Scaled Score: | | 16 | 17 | 14 |
|     Block Design—Scaled Score: | | 13 | 12 | 13 |
| 4) WRAT | | | | |
|     Reading—Grade Equivalent: | 2.3 | 3.9 | 4.8 | 6.6 |
|     Spelling—Grade Equivalent: | 2.0 | 3.2 | 3.7 | 5.4 |
|     Arithmetic—Grade Equivalent | 2.6 | | 2.4 | 3.9 |
| Non-Standardized: | | | | |
| 1) Labeling Task based on | | | | |
|     WISC-R Picture Completion Items | | | | |
|     Raw Score | | 22 | 21 | 21 |
| 2) Learning Lab Language Scale | | | | |
|     (telling a story to a picture) | | | | |
|     Raw Scores: | | | | |
|     Function | 3 | | 4 | 6 |
|     Syntax | 3 | | 7 | 5 |
|     Cognitive Style | 2 | | 2 | 6 |
|     Willingness to Communicate | 3 | | 3 | 5 |

Street I feel they think about the needs of kids, and that "you can do it."

Perhaps the technique is less important than the sense of caring and that you believe in him.

His second-grade teacher stated, "Now he's very confident about himself. Even when he's with other children who read better, he'll volunteer right away."

His third-grade teacher said, "Good year generally—adjusted well to class, though quiet at first."

# CHAPTER 10

# Case Study III:
# A Shy Little Fellow

---

## JILL/BRIAN DYAD

*The Graduate-Student Tutor: Jill*

Jill is a mature woman who is introspective and somewhat verbally guarded in her contacts with others, particularly in terms of her personal life. She is highly intelligent and witty. There is a slight tinge of cynicism on the surface. But underneath, if one is fortunate enough to know her well (and this is not easy), one finds enormous sensitivity, warmth, and a beautiful, almost naive sentimentality. Although she has much insight into herself and others, she is often reluctant to express herself, particularly in the presence of more assertive person-

---

Much of this case study was prepared by the supervisor and graduate-student tutor.

alities. One gets the feeling that her silence is in no way a withdrawal. She is a keen observer and listener, rare qualities that are extremely valuable in her work.

She chooses her words carefully and is low-keyed and gentle in her approach to children. She has about her at times an air of sadness. She is realistically self-questioning and self-critical and responds positively to suggestions without in any way feeling threatened. If anything, she is somewhat hard on herself, forever searching for a better way and asking of herself how she might have done better.

She is highly organized and structured without being rigid and is, in fact, flexible and spontaneous. She is able to shift gears, to seize the moment, and to use it creatively to teach. She has an impressive ability to take advantage of an unexpected happening and to turn it into a learning experience.

Jill was born in England and spent time teaching elementary school there. She graduated from Columbia University having majored in English and had completed her course work at Bank Street. Her independent study was to be a case study of Brian and she would supervise in the Practicum the following semester. Her fieldwork was with normal five- and six-year-olds at a therapeutic nursery. She also did volunteer work with emotionally disturbed preschool children. She had recently just begun privately tutoring children with learning problems.

She took the Practicum with the hope of gaining more knowledge and experience in working with learning-disabled children. She felt that in order to grow professionally, since most of her background had been with emotionally disturbed youngsters, she needed to focus more directly on the processes of learning and on techniques of dealing with deviations in these processes.

## Type of Child Desired

Jill expressed the desire to work with a child with reading problems. At the time of her first interview with Brian she sensed an immediate rapport. There seemed to me to be a mutual attraction between this very small and soft-spoken child (who exhibited a quality of helplessness) and this very soft-spoken, nurturing woman.

*The Child: Brian*

There are many children like Brian, who is seven years old. His moods and, indeed, his very tempo shift dramatically. Environmental factors greatly influence these shifts. Thus, the description of Brian will be in terms of his behavior in a supportive and structured situation, which Jill provided.

*Physical Appearance:* Small (appears physically like a five-year-old, handsome, neatly dressed).
*Temperament:* Highly focused (one-to-one setting), persistent, perfectionistic—sometimes overly. (This interacted with his feelings of inadequacy and produced defeatism with withdrawal). Distractible in overly stimulating situations (observed at first party).
*Affect—Emotional Development:* Frequent mood shifts: on one hand, fearful, passive, afraid to risk involvement, little eye contact; on the other hand, open, spontaneous, charming, good eye contact. Shifts from aggressive to regressive (infantile), from helplessness to independence. Asks many significant questions of Jill (feels free to do so). He's like his tutor and is a questioner.
*Social:* Difficulty relating to peers; competitive (has expressed feelings of inadequacy due to his size); generally relates to adults with caution but is at times surprisingly open.
*Expressive Language:* Articulation difficulties (delayed development); infantile quality and syntax. This is not consistent. Sometimes extremely sophisticated. Passive quality but sometimes very expressive and spontaneous.
*Receptive Language:* Excellent ability to follow directions.
*Concepts:* Excellent number concepts; able to categorize, predict logically, and generalize. Some concrete thinking evidenced.
*Gross Motor:* Awkward, clumsy gate.
*Fine Motor* (right-handed): Extreme tension in pencil grip; needs to put much energy and effort in fine motor tasks.
*Auditory Modality:* Difficulty discriminating short vowel sounds. Auditory sequential memory; possible processing difficulties.
*Visual:* Some weakness noted in visual memory.
*Academic Development:* Strong in math concepts (2.5-5/78 PIAT Math); reading and spelling poor (comprehension good); poor sight vocabulary. Began as non-reader; now able to decode simple three-letter linguistic patterns (mat, men, cap). Reading at first-grade level; has developed some sight vocabulary.

*Family Background*

Bit by bit in their early weeks together Jill learned some of the details of Brian's history. Much of this was revealed to Jill by Brian's teacher who became increasingly communicative with her.

Brian is an adopted child. Information about his biological family and prenatal history is not available. It is assumed by the teacher that he is the product of an interracial union. His adoptive parents are white. There are two older natural children. Brian was adopted at a time when the marriage was undergoing many difficulties, and it was hoped that the new baby would bring the couple closer together. Such was not the case and the marriage ended in divorce. Brian's father, who was a physician, remarried and all of the children spent time with him and his new wife. A few years ago Brian's adoptive father committed suicide by injecting himself with an overdose of demerol. Brian and his siblings still maintain contact with the second wife of the adoptive father. This is reportedly a positive relationship. Interviews with his adoptive mother revealed that she is not certain as to whether or not Brian knows that he was adopted. Additionally, it is her belief that all of the children think that their father's death was an accident. Our own contacts with Brian lead us to the opinion that his awareness of these very loaded issues is keen, albeit confused. Moreover, his many conversations with Jill involving the subject of racial differences indicate much concern regarding his own identity.

*The Pairing*

Jill's level of maturity, her ability to wait, observe, and reflect, and her natural spontaneity and enthusiasm made a good match with Brian's need for perfectionism and high level of motivation. His distractibilty matched well with her excellent attention span and concentration.

*The Process*

Jill's priority was, of course, to establish a warm and trusting relationship with Brian. She immediately sensed his fearfulness of relating to others and the careful distance that he kept. She accepted this without feeling rejected, and respected his need to defend himself in this manner. In order to better understand this very complicated child, she began to assess his weaknesses, his strengths, and his style with a variety of innovative and nonthreatening activities.

*Example.* Brian had been playing with the miniature toy animals that are part of the several beautiful games that Jill devised. She was interested in determining his dominance and asked him to pretend that he was a hunter who was out shooting wild animals. She rolled up a piece of paper, telling him that this was his spyglass. She asked him to close his eyes while she hid some of the small animals about the room. Then she asked him to put the spyglass to his eye and to try to find the animals. He thoroughly enjoyed the game as he did the pretend football game that followed (in which he passed and kicked an imaginary ball). With these nonthreatening activities, Jill was able to get a great deal of information.

## Evaluation of Pediatrician

1) Maturational delay (generally at six-year-old level); delayed motorically (gross and fine motor delayed); overflow in motor tasks.
2) Brian might have been a premature high-risk infant. This combined with environmental problems may be a significant factor in the child's development.
3) Well-focused, persistent, and well-related during interview.

## The Tutorials

Jill exhibited both flexibility and structure. Her planning was well-organized and creative. Each session was linked to the next so that the entire year was beautifully and appropriately coordinated. She recognized Brian's need for repetition and reinforcement and developed a variety of entertaining and nonthreatening activities to provide him with this. She is low-keyed and warm. She makes beautiful original materials. She chooses her words carefully and knows the value of silence (she does not feel the need to keep up the verbal interaction, recognizing that well-placed silence is very positive). She is very sensitive to Brian's needs and quick to pick up on his verbal and nonverbal clues. Her timing is beautiful. She does not rush in impulsively, but weighs her actions and words with care. She is aware of the child's emotional difficulties and uses great control and discretion so as not to open up a Pandora's box.

Brian and Jill both possess and appreciate a sense of humor. They work seriously together but they have a wonderful ability to play. (They frequently sing together to reduce tension.)

Jill was aware of what caused Brian anxiety, and she structured their sessions in a way which reduced the possibility of the occurrence of such anxiety. She is able to help him to shift to another activity without being arbitrary.

Her maturity, her wisdom, her orientation, her restraint, and her spontaneity combined to make the tutorials of tremendous impact and value to both Jill and Brian.

*Videotapes*

The videotapes exemplified all of what has been described. In the composite it is particularly interesting to trace the growth of trust between the two (the change in Brian's affect and his increased eye contact). The tapes clearly convey the quality of their interaction and the importance of their relationship. Observing these tapes, one becomes aware of Jill's timing and sensitive choice of words.

Brian's language patterns and his mood contrasts are highly visible in the tapes. He has problems with aggression, fears about death, concern with his size, and academic inadequacies.

Jill's ability to stand back and allow Brian space and silence is dramatically illustrated in the segment where he looked at the book without words.

*Counseling Brian's Mother*

Mother was not too available because she was working. Efforts were made with her employer to have her released a few times during the year. On these visits, videotapes of Brian working with Jill were used for discussions of Brian's behavior and for Mother to make some simple changes in her management of the child. On occasion, Jill would visit the home so that she could chat with Brian and his mother and model the desired behavior.

*Log*

Jill's log reflects the quality and content of her work as well as the growth of a beautiful relationship. Jill, throughout her log, asks many important questions. She is self-critical and recognizes when she has "goofed." At the same time she has faith in her ability to grow and immediately suggests what she will do about her "goof" (her word). In reading the log, one finds oneself both laughing and crying. Her work is integrated and creative. The therapeutic nature of this relationship is clear, as is the educational. One does not often have the opportunity to see such beautiful balance. Here are some excerpts.

Growth of Insights
   *2nd Session*
Jill observes the beginning of the "silly" behavior which frequently occurred during their sessions: "When certain tasks are presented in which Brian feels insecure, the silliness occurs." Jill picks up his frustration and talks directly with him about it.
   *5th Session*
Jill notes, "When he gets into an area where he is not so sure of himself, he becomes more impulsive and as he begins to do poorly, the anxiety grows and the impulsivity increases."
"My feeling is that he is in need of and wants structure and responds well to it. I'm sure from seeing his reactions to other boys that in the classroom he is constantly aware of and interacting with the other kids and thus cannot focus on any task."

Sensitivity to Brian's Needs and Style
   *6th Session*
Jill asks if she should finish a story she's been reading or whether she should stop and finish it next week: "He wants to finish now. I feel his need to end something appropriately is a good indication of his own sense of order and will be a valuable asset in his learning process."
Noting his interest in labels and in being read to, she says, "I'm sure he wants very much to read."

Awareness of Brian's Need for Success
"I told him that I had heard something fantastic about him from

A. with whom he had met last week. I told him that I knew he could read some words and how great that was. I told him that I had made him a book and that I had the feeling he would read all the words in it." (She shows him the book of the "At" family. She knew he could read this.) "He read it all and I said, "Brian, you've been holding out on me.' I tickled him in the tummy. I often put my arm around his shoulder and tussled his hair and he accepts that. But this time he giggled and seemed pleased by this physical contact."

Self-criticism and Self-awareness
"This, I'm afraid, was a real mistake on my part and I'm angry with myself that I was being so precious about my materials. It would have been so good for him to have had it [something Brian had made in a former session that he wanted to take with him], but I will make him "Dan the Man' next week. I can only hope I didn't miss my chance." "I forgot some of my materials and as I was looking through my things I said, 'What a dummy I am to have forgotten the paper.' In a very quiet voice Brian said, 'You're not a dummy.' I really did not hear this until I'd played my tapes of the session and was struck by the sadness in Brian's tone when he said it.
"I told him how proud I was that he knows so many words and how well he'd done in reading two whole books; 'That's very good,' I said. On the tape I heard a very faint 'no.' He obviously does not feel at all good about himself."

Development of Trust
"I gave him a book which he had read the week before knowing how much he enjoys repeating things that he succeeded at. [She doesn't tell him he's wrong when he makes a mistake but rather she provides him with a strategy, a way of correcting himself.]
"When he made a mistake and said "Nan' for "Nat,' I pointed to the *T* and said that the last letter is important and it's important to look at all the letters. Then he self-corrected.
"Back at school Brian says that he can go back to his classroom by himself. I said it was a rule we had to take the kids all the way back to the classroom. I did not want him to think I did not trust him. . . ."

Growth of Insight into the Ways He Operates
She is able to pick up on the behavioral clues that he gives in regard to his emotional needs and he comes more and more aware of his vulnerability. She asks, "When should I step in? How

much should I talk about these things?" She doesn't impulsively rush in. She knows the importance of choosing her words carefully.

Jill goes on to say, "With such a poor self-image it is to be expected that Brian will find it hard to accept compliments. Does one just pour them on whenever they are appropriate or should I talk to him about this? I feel he might be willing to hear."

Jill's Ability to Utilize Every Aspect of the Learning Situation

During a rhyming game, they were working with words with *all* at the end. They arrived at the word *tall*. Jill notes, "I asked if he knew what tall was and asked how tall is Brian? Brian replied, 'Little.' I said, 'You're not; let's measure you.' Brian replied, 'I want to be big.' " Jill had a tape measure (she was prepared for this). She measured him and wrote it down—4'2". They both read this several times: "He was very subdued." Jill asks in the log, "Is his teasing of big boys related to feelings of smallness?"

Therapeutic Nature of Relationship Grows
Jill Uses Bibliotherapy

She reads to him at almost every session and does not question him about the story but rather allows him to listen and think it through himself. She read such books as "Crow Boy," "Two's A Team," "There's A Nightmare in my Closet."

The therapeutic alliance that developed between adult and child and the sensitivity and awareness of the adult provided the insights and strategies that enhanced growth through the emotional, experiential, and cognitive channels, integrating all aspects of treatment.

# Appendix A

---

Please prepare a chart listing *one* salient strength and weakness for each of the dimensions we have discussed. Use the model below to organize the information about your child.

|  | *Strengths* | *Weaknesses* |
|---|---|---|
| PHYSICAL (MOTOR/SPEECH) |  |  |
| TEMPERAMENT |  |  |
| AFFECT |  |  |
| PERCEPTION |  |  |
| COGNITION/LANGUAGE |  |  |
| SOCIAL |  |  |
| ACADEMIC SKILLS |  |  |

Write a short summary paragraph here on implications re direction and focus for upcoming sessions.

# Appendix B

SCALE I

TRAIT ANALYSIS OF CHARACTERISTICS OF TUTORS

1. PERSONALITY *(Affect)*
   strong ego (acceptance of self) ...weak ego (low self-esteem)
   respectful control (tolerant
       and firm) .........................arbitrary control
   supportive and emphatic ..........authoritarian and critical
   appropriate assertiveness .........manipulative or submissive
   enthusiastic ..........................lack of enthusiasm
   allows for initiative
       and autonomy ...................intrusive

2. TEMPERAMENT
   moderate rhythm ..................slow or fast-paced
   appropriate amount of stimuli ...under- or over-stimulated
   reflective .............................impulsive
   focused ...............................distracted
   perseveres ...........................gives up easily
   flexible-adaptive ...................rigid

3. COGNITIVE STYLE
   organized ............................fragmented
   creative ..............................stereotypic

4. CLARITY OF VERBALIZATION
   clarity of words .....................lack of clarity
   appropriate level of syntax .......confused and inappropriate level
       of syntax
   appropriate and clear concepts ..confused and inappropriate con-
       cepts

## TREATMENT ALLIANCE RESEARCH

### Personality (Affect)

| | 5 | 4 | 3 | 2 | 1 | 0 | |
|---|---|---|---|---|---|---|---|
| Strong ego (acceptance of self) | | | | | | | Weak ego (low self-esteem) |
| Respectful control (tolerant and firm) | | | | | | | Arbitrary control |
| Supportive and empathic | | | | | | | Authoritarian and critical |
| Appropriate assertiveness | | | | | | | Manipulative or submissive |
| Enthusiastic | | | | | | | Lack of enthusiasm |
| Allows for initiative and autonomy | | | | | | | Intrusive |

Name of Tape _____ Date on Tape _____

Numbers on Tape: _____ to _____

Beginning with: _____ Ending with: _____

_____

Researcher's Name                    Date

## TREATMENT ALLIANCE RESEARCH

### Temperament

| | 5 | 4 | 3 | 2 | 1 | 0 | |
|---|---|---|---|---|---|---|---|
| Moderate rhythm | | | | | | | Slow- or fast-paced |
| Appropriate amount of stimuli | | | | | | | Under- or over-stimulated |
| Reflective | | | | | | | Impulsive |
| Focused | | | | | | | Distracted |
| Perseveres | | | | | | | Gives up easily |
| Flexible-adaptive | | | | | | | Rigid |

### Cognitive Style

| | 5 | 4 | 3 | 2 | 1 | 0 | |
|---|---|---|---|---|---|---|---|
| Organized | | | | | | | Fragmented |
| Creative | | | | | | | Stereotypic |

### Clarity of Verbalization

| | 5 | 4 | 3 | 2 | 1 | 0 | |
|---|---|---|---|---|---|---|---|
| Clarity of words | | | | | | | Lack of clarity |
| Appropriate level of syntax | | | | | | | Confused and inappropriate level of syntax |
| Appropriate and clear concepts | | | | | | | Confused and inappropriate concepts |

# Appendix C

---

TRAIT ANALYSIS OF CHARACTERISTICS OF CHILDREN

1. PERSONALITY *(Affect)*
   strong ego (acceptance of self) ...weak ego (low self-esteem)
   control of own behavior ...........arbitrary control
   high frustration tolerance .........low frustration tolerance
   appropriate assertiveness ..........manipulative or submissive
   enthusiasm ...........................lack of enthusiasm
   attentive ..............................withdrawn
   shows initiative and autonomy ..intrusive-negative

2. TEMPERAMENT
   moderate rhythm ...................slow or fast paced
   need for low stimulation ..........need for high stimulation
      to activate                         to activate
   reflective .............................impulsive
   perseveres ...........................gives up easily
   flexibility ............................rigidity
   attention (focus) ...................distractible (unfocused)

3. COGNITIVE STYLE
   organized ............................fragmented
   adaptable ...........................nonadaptable
   innovative ...........................stereotyped

4. CLARITY OF VERBALIZATION
   clarity with words ..................lack of clarity
   appropriate use of words .........inappropriate use of words
   appropriate use of concepts ......inappropriate or confused
      (concrete vs. abstract)             concepts

179

# TREATMENT ALLIANCE RESEARCH

### Personality (Affect)

|  | 5 | 4 | 3 | 2 | 1 | 0 |  |
|---|---|---|---|---|---|---|---|
| Strong Ego (acceptance of self) |  |  |  |  |  |  | Weak ego (low self-esteem) |
| Control of own behavior |  |  |  |  |  |  | Arbitrary control |
| High frustration tolerance |  |  |  |  |  |  | Low frustration tolerance |
| Appropriate assertiveness |  |  |  |  |  |  | Manipulative or submissive |
| Enthusiasm |  |  |  |  |  |  | Lack of enthusiasm |
| Attentive |  |  |  |  |  |  | Withdrawn |
| Shows initiative and autonomy |  |  |  |  |  |  | Intrusive-negative |

Name of Tape _____ Date on Tape _____

Numbers on Tape: _____ to _____

Beginning with: _____ Ending with: _____

_____

Researcher's Name                              Date

## TREATMENT ALLIANCE RESEARCH

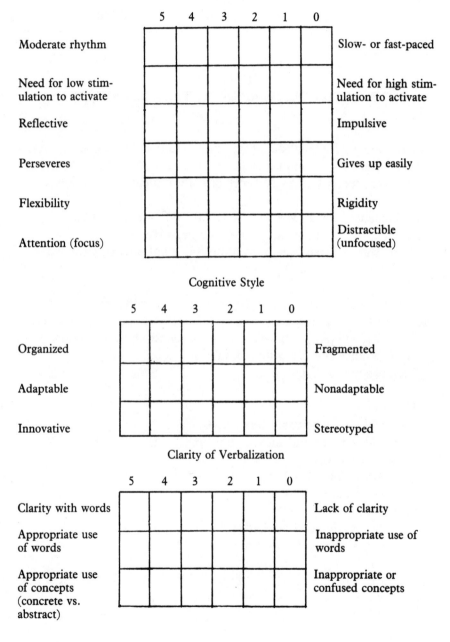

Temperament

|  | 5 | 4 | 3 | 2 | 1 | 0 |  |
|---|---|---|---|---|---|---|---|
| Moderate rhythm | | | | | | | Slow- or fast-paced |
| Need for low stim-ulation to activate | | | | | | | Need for high stim-ulation to activate |
| Reflective | | | | | | | Impulsive |
| Perseveres | | | | | | | Gives up easily |
| Flexibility | | | | | | | Rigidity |
| Attention (focus) | | | | | | | Distractible (unfocused) |

Cognitive Style

|  | 5 | 4 | 3 | 2 | 1 | 0 |  |
|---|---|---|---|---|---|---|---|
| Organized | | | | | | | Fragmented |
| Adaptable | | | | | | | Nonadaptable |
| Innovative | | | | | | | Stereotyped |

Clarity of Verbalization

|  | 5 | 4 | 3 | 2 | 1 | 0 |  |
|---|---|---|---|---|---|---|---|
| Clarity with words | | | | | | | Lack of clarity |
| Appropriate use of words | | | | | | | Inappropriate use of words |
| Appropriate use of concepts (concrete vs. abstract) | | | | | | | Inappropriate or confused concepts |

# Appendix D

SCALE III

INTERACTIVE MEASURE OF MUTUAL RESPONSIVITY

This measure records the positive and negative communications between the graduate-student tutor and child in a time sequence. Each line represents a communication in time and allows one to see the mutual responsivity in three types of communication as follows:

Movement toward (M+) or away (M−) from each other.
Facial expression—positive (F+) or negative (F−)
Verbalizations that have a meaningful, emotional or supportive content—positive (V+) or negative (V−).

Each variable was studied separately and recorded separately. Movement and facial expressions were coded without sound when playing back the videotape. Verbalizations were coded last with sound so as not to influence the other two variables.

Examples are as follows:

*Movement*
  • child moves toward tutor (M+)
  • child gets up and moves about room (M−)
*Facial Expression*
  • tutor smiles (F+)
  • child frowns (F−)
*Verbalization*
  • "I'm really good at that" (V+)
  • "I don't know how—I'm stupid" (V−)

Any pause was recorded by skipping a line. Introduction of a new subject was recorded by skipping a line.

## TREATMENT ALLIANCE RESEARCH
## MEASURES OF INTERACTIONS: MOVEMENT

Name of Tape _____ Date _____

Numbers on Tape _____ to _____

Beginning with words: "_____"

Ending with words: "_____"

| Child | — MOVEMENT — | Adult |
|-------|--------------|-------|
| | | |

## TREATMENT ALLIANCE RESEARCH
## MEASURES OF INTERACTIONS: FACIAL EXPRESSIONS

Name of Tape _____ Date _____

Numbers on Tape _____ to _____

Beginning with words: "_____"

Ending with words: "_____"

| Child | — MOVEMENT — | Adult |
|-------|--------------|-------|
|       |              |       |

## TREATMENT ALLIANCE RESEARCH
## MEASURES OF INTERACTIONS: VERBALIZATIONS

Name of Tape _____ Date _____

Numbers on Tape _____ to _____

Beginning with words: "_____"

Ending with words: "_____"

Child            — MOVEMENT —            Adult

# References

Adelman, H. S. Remedial classroom instruction revisited. *Journal of Special Education*, 1971, *5*(4), 311-322.

Allen, K. E., Henke L. B., Harris, F. R., Baer, D. M., & Reynolds, N. J. Control of hyperactivity by social reinforcement of attending behavior. *Journal of Educational Psychology*, 1967, *58*, 231-237.

Anastasi, A. Heredity, environment and the question, "How?" *Psychological Review*, 1958, *65*(4), 197-208.

Ayres, S. Patterns of perceptual-motor dysfunction in children. *Perceptual and Motor Skills* (Monograph Supplement), 1965, *1*(20), 335-368.

Barkley, R. A. The use of psychopharmacology to study reciprocal influences in parent-child interaction. *Journal of Abnormal Child Psychology*, 1981, *9*, 303-310.

Barrish, H. H., Saunder, M., & Wolf, M. Good behavior game: Effects of individual contingencies for group consequences on disruptive behavior in the classroom. *Journal of Applied Behavior Analysis*, 1969, *2*, 119-124.

Bates, S. E., & Pettit, G. S. Adult individual differences as moderators of child effects. *Journal of Abnormal Child Psychology*, 1981, *9*, 329-340.

Bell, R. Q. Stimulus control of parent or caretaker behavior by offspring. *Developmental Psychology*, 1971, *4*, 63-72.

187

Bell, R. Q. Parent, child and reciprocal influences. *American Psychologist*, October 1979, 821-826.

Biber, B. Distinguished research scholar, emeritus. Conference, *Roots of Excellence*, Bank Street College of Education, New York City, 1954.

Biber, B. Schooling as an influence in developing healthy personality. In R. Kotinsky & H. Witmer (Eds.), *Community programs for mental health*. Cambridge, MA: Harvard University Press, 1955, 158-221.

Biber, B. A learning teaching paradigm integrating intellectual and affective processes. In E. M. Bower and W. G. Hollister (Eds.), *Behavioral science frontiers in education*. New York: John Wiley, 1967, 111-155.

Birch, H., & Lefford, A. Intersensory development in children. *Monograph of Social Research in Child Development*, 28(5), 1963.

Blackmer, G. W. The contribution made to student achievement by the degree of cognitive style match between tutors and students. (Doctoral dissertation, University of Florida, 1981.) *Dissertation Abstracts International*, 1981, 41(9-A), 3853.

Bloom, B. S. Taxonomy of educational objectives. *Handbook I: The cognitive domain*. New York: David McKay, 1956.

Bloom, B. S. *Stability and change in human characteristics*. New York: John Wiley, 1964.

Brazelton, B. T., & Als, H. Four early stages in the development of mother-infant interactions. Helen Ross Lecture, Chicago Psychoanalytic Society, Chicago, April 13, 1978.

Brent, D. E., & Routh, D. K. Response cost and impulsive word recognition errors in reading disabled children. *Journal of Abnormal Child Psychology*, 1978, b, 211-219.

Brown, R. The effects of congruency between learning style and teaching style on college student achievement. College student journal, California State University, 1978.

Bruner, J. *Toward a theory of instruction*. Cambridge, MA: Harvard University Press, 1966.

Bruner, S. G. Processes of growth in infancy in stimulation. In A. Ambrose (Ed.), *Stimulation in early infancy*. London: Academic Press, 1969.

Carr, J. E., & Posthuma, A. The role of cognitive process in social interaction (Journal article, University of Washington, 1975.) *International Journal of Social Psychiatry*, 1975, 21(3), 157-165.

Carroll, A. W. The classroom as an eco-system. *Focus on Exceptional Children*, 1974, 6, 1-11.

Cartwright, G. P., Cartwright, C. A., & Ysseldyke, J. E. Two decision models: Identification and diagnostic teaching of handicapped children in the regular classroom. *Psychology in the Schools*, 1973, 10, 4-11.

Chapman, M. Isolating casual effects through experimental changes in parent-child interaction. *Journal of Abnormal Child Psychology*, 1981, 9, 321-327.

Chess, S. Temperament in the normal infant. In J. Hellmuth (Ed.), *Exceptional infant. Volume I, The normal infant*. New York: Brunner/Mazel, 1967.

Chomsky, N. Recent contributions to the theory of innate ideas. In S. Sapir and A. Nitzburg (Eds.), *Children with learning problems*. New York: Brunner/Mazel, 1973, 99-108.

Cole, M., John-Steiner, V., Scribner, S., & Souberman, E., (Eds). *Mind and society: L. S. Vygotsky*. Cambridge, MA: Harvard University Press, 1978.

Coles, R. *Erik H. Erikson, the growth of his work.* Boston: Atlantic, Little, Brown, 1970.

Collins, M. A. An investigation of the influences of interpersonal compatibility on pupil achievement and teacher and pupil perceptions of the relationship. (Doctoral dissertation, University of Rochester, 1970). *Dissertation Abstracts International*, 1970, *31*(4-A), 1614-1615.

Cravioto, J. Nutritional deprivation and psychological development in children. Deprivation and Psychological Development (*A Report of the Pan American Conference of the World Health Organization*), 1966, *134*, 38-54.

Cravioto, J., & Arrieta, R. The effect of added systematic stimulation on the mental recovery of severely malnourished infants less than six months old. *Pediatrics*, 1981.

Cravioto, J., DeLicardie, E. R., & Birch, A. G. Nutrition, growth and intersensory development. *Pediatrics* (Supplement), 1966, *38*(2,2), 319-372.

Cravioto, J., & Robles, B. The influence of protein-calorie malnutrition on psychological behavior. *American Journal of Orthopsychiatry*, 1965, *35*, 449.

Cruickshank, W., Bentzen, F., Ratzburg, F., & Tannhauser, M. *A teaching method for brain-injured and hyperactive children*, Syracuse, NY: Syracuse University Press, 1961.

De Hirsch, K. Interactions between educational therapists and child. *Bulletin of the Orton Society*, 1977, *XXVII*, 88-101.

Deutsch, C. Education for disadvantaged groups. *Review of Educational Research*, 1965, *35*(2), 140-146.

Dewey, J. Presidential address to the conference of the American Psychological Association, 1899.

Dewey, J. *Experience and education.* New York: Collier Publications, 1963.

Erikson, E. H. Problems of infancy and childhood. In M. S. E. Senn (Ed.), Symposium on the Healthy Personality, *Transactions of Fourth Conference*, March 1950. New York: Josiah Macy Jr. Foundation.

Eysenck, H. J. Learning theory and behavior therapy. *Journal of Mental Science*, 1959, *105*, 61-75.

Federal Register. *Children with specific learning disabilities: Definition.* Washington, D.C.: U.S. Office of Education, February 20, 1975.

Field, T. The three R's of infant-adult interactions: Rhythms, repertories and responsivity. *Journal of Pediatric Psychology*, 1978, *3*, 131-136.

Forehand, R., & Baumeister, A. A. Effects of variations in auditory-visual stimulation on activity levels of severe mental retardates. *American Journal of Mental Deficiency*, 1970, *74*, 470-474.

Fraiberg, S. Blind infants and their mothers: An examination of the sign system. In M. Lewis & L. A. Rosenblum (Eds.), *The effect of the infant on its caregiver.* New York: Wiley, 1974.

Frandsen, K. D., & Rosenfeld, L. B. Fundamental interpersonal relations orientations in dyads: An empirical analysis of Schultz's FIRO-B as an index of compatibility (Journal article, Pennsylvania State University, 1973). *Speech Monographs*, 1973, *40*(2), 113-122.

Freeman, R. D. Emotional reactions of handicapped children. *Rehabilitation Literature*, 1967, *28*(9), 274-281.

Freud, A. *The ego and the mechanisms of defense.* New York: International University Press, 1946.

Freud, A. *Psychoanalysis for teachers-parents.* New York: Emerson Books, 1947.

Freud, A. The role of the teacher. *Harvard Educational Review,* 1952, *22,* 4.

Freud, A. Presentation to world organization for early childhood education. *Report of the 9th World Assembly,* London, July 16-21, 1962.

Freud, A. The concept of developmental lines. *Psychoanalytic Study of the Child,* 1963, *18,* 245-265.

Freud, S. *An outline of psychoanalysis.* New York: Norton, 1949.

Freud, S. In J. Strachey (Ed.), *The standard edition of the complete psychological works.* London: Hogarth Press, 1953.

Frostig, M. *Developmental test of visual perception.* Palo Alto, CA: Consulting Psychological Press, 1961.

Fry, P. S., & Charron, P. A. The effects of cognitive style and counselor client compatibility on client growth. (Journal article, University of Calgary, Canada, 1980). *Journal of Counseling Psychology,* 1980, *27*(6), 529-538.

Gagne, R. M. *Conditions of learning* (2nd. ed.). New York: Holt, Rinehart and Winston, 1971.

Gardner, R. W. Evolution and brain injury. *Bulletin of Menninger Clinic,* 1971, *35*(2).

Gates, G. D. Student teachers and cooperating teachers: An exploratory study of individual characteristics, compatibility and their relationship to success in student teaching. (Doctoral dissertation, University of Wisconsin, 1978.) *Dissertation Abstracts International,* 1978, *38*(10-A), 6067-6068.

Gesell, A. Maturation and infant behavior patterns. *Psychological Review,* 1929, *36,* 307-319.

Gesell, A. *Studies in child development.* New York: Harper, 1948.

Gesell, A., & Ilg., F. L. *Infant and child in the culture of today.* New York: Harper, 1943.

Gesell, A., & Thompson, H. Twins t & c from infancy to adolescence. *Genetic Psychology Monograph,* 1941, *24,* 3-121.

Glaser, R. Individuals and learning: The new aptitude. *Educational Researcher,* 1972, *1,* 5-13.

Glidewell, J. C. On the analysis of social intervention. In J. C. Glidewell (Ed.), *Parental attitudes and child behavior.* Springfield, IL: Charles C Thomas, 1961.

Goldstein, K. *After-effects of braifn injuries in war.* New York: Grune & Stratton, 1942.

Gottman, J. *Marital interaction: Experimental investigations.* New York: Academic Press, 1979.

Gourevitch, A. Encounter and communication. *Contemporary Psychoanalysis,* 1982, *18*(2) 282-290.

Greenspan, S. I., & Liberman, A. F. Infants, mothers and their interactions: A quantitative clinical approach to developmental assessment. In S. I. Greenspan & Pollack (Eds.), *The course of life: Psychoanalytic contributions toward understanding personality development, Vol. I: Infancy and early childhood,* Bethesda, MD: National Institute of Mental Health, 1980, pp. 271-311.

Harper, L. U. The young as a source of stimuli controlling caretaker behavior. *Developmental Psychology,* 1971, *4,* 73-88.

Hartman, H. Comments on the psychoanalytic theory of the ego. *Psychoanalytic Study of the Child,* 1950, *5,* 74-96.

Hebb, D. O. *Organization of behavior.* New York: Wiley, 1949.

Hebb, D. O. Drive and the c.n.s. (conceptual nervous system). *Psychological Review,* 1955, *62,* 243-254.

Hess, E. H. Imprinting. *Science*, 1959, *130*, 133-141.

Holzman, P. S. *Psychoanalysis and psychopathology*. New York: McGraw-Hill, 1970.

Hopkins, B. L., Schutte, R. C., & Gorton, K. L. The effects of access to a playroom on the rate and quality of printing and writing of first and second-grade students. *Journal of Applied Behavior Analysis*, 1971, *4*, 77-87.

Hunt, J. McV. *Intelligence and experience*. New York: Ronald Press, 1961.

Hunt, J. M. Toward a theory of guided learning in development. In R. H. Ojemann & K. Pritchett (Eds.), *Giving emphasis to guided learning*. Cleveland, OH: Educational Research Council, 1966.

Hunt, J. McV. *The challenge of incompetence and poverty*. Urbana, IL: University of Illinois Press, 1969.

Hurst, J. A. Relationship of client satisfaction and client progress in therapy to similarities of counselor-client interpersonal values (Doctoral dissertation, Ball State University, 1979). *Dissertation Abstracts International*, 1979, *40*(4-A), 1875-1876.

*ITPA (Illinois Test of Psycholinguistic Ability)*. Urbana: University of Illinois Press, 1961.

Johnson, D. Learning disabilities. Paper presented at the meeting of American Psychological Association, Washington D.C., September 1976.

Johnson, H. *Children in the nursery school*. New York: John Day, 1928.

Josselyn, I. *Psychosocial development of children*. New York: Family Service Association of America, 1948.

Kahn, E., & Cohen, L. C. Organic drivenness, a brain-stem syndrome and an experience. *New England Journal of Medicine*, 1943, *210*, 748-752.

Kaufman, J. Match or mismatch of cognitive styles in vocational counseling dyadic interactions (Doctoral dissertation, University of Iowa, 1979). *Dissertation Abstracts International*, 1979, *39*(12-A), 7162-7163.

Kephart, N. C. Learning disability: An educational adventure. *The Kappa Delta Pi Lecture Series*, 1968.

Koffka, K. Special features of mental growth. In R. W. Marks (Ed.), *Great ideas in psychology*. New York: Bantam Books, 1966, pp. 171-251.

Laurendeau, M., & Pinard, A. *Casual thinking in the child*. New York: International Universities Press, 1963.

Lerner, J. W. Systems analysis and special education. *Journal of Special Education*, 1973, *7*, 15-26.

Lewis, M., & Lee-Painter, S. An interactional approach to the mother-infant dyad. In M. Lewis & L. A. Rosenblum (Eds.), *The effect of the infant on its caregiver*. New York: Wiley, 1974.

Lipsitt, I. The pleasures and annoyances of infants: Approach and avoidance. In E. B. Tolman (Ed.), *Social responsiveness of infants*. Hillsdale, NJ: Lawrence Erlbaum Associates, 1979.

Livanov, M. N., Gavrilova, N. A., & Aslanov, A. S. Correlation of bio-potentials in human frontal lobes. In A. R. Luria & E. D. Homskaya (Eds.), *Frontal lobes and regulation of psychological processes*. Moscow: Moscow University Press, 1966.

Luria, A. R. *The nature of human conflict*. New York: Liveright, 1932.

Luria. A. R. Verbal regulation of behavior. In M. A. B. Brazier (Ed.), *The central nervous system and behavior*. New York: Josiah Macy Jr. Foundation, 1960.

Luria, A. R. *The role of speech in the regulation of normal and abnormal behavior*. Oxford: Pergamon Press, 1961.

Luria, A. R. *The man with a shattered world*. New York: Basic Books, 1972.

Luria, A. R. The origin and cerebral organization of man's conscious action. In S. Sapir and A. Nitzburg (Eds.), *Children with learning problems*, New York: Brunner/Mazel, 1973, 109-130.

Luria, A. R. *Cognitive development: Its cultural and social* Cambridge, MA: Harvard University Press, 1976.

Luria, A. R., & Homskaya, E. D. (Eds.). *Frontal lobes and regulationn of psychological processes*. Moscow: Moscow University Press, 1966.

Malloy, T. E. The relationship between therapist-client interpersonal compatibility, sex therapist, and therapeutic outcome (Journal article, New Mexico State University, 1981). *Journal of Clinical Psychology*, 1981, *37*(2), 316-322.

Mann, L., & Sabatino, D. (Eds.). *The first review of special education*. Philadelphia: JSE Press, 1973.

Masland, R. L. *Brain mechanisms*. Paper presented to the Orton Society. Rockefeller University, New York City, October, 1966.

Masland, R. L. Children with minimal brain dysfunction—a national problem. In T. Tarnpol (Ed.), *Learning disabilities: Introduction to educational and medical management*. Springfield, IL: Charles C Thomas, 1969.

Maslow, A. H. *Motivation and personality*. New York: Harper, 1954.

Maves, P. A. Roommate matching as a function of similarity: An application of nonmetric analysis to formulate a matching process for clinical research (Doctoral dissertation, University of Colorado, 1983). *Dissertation Abstracts International*, 1979, *39*(11-B), 5569.

McClintock, R. A. The therapeutic relationship and outcomes of speech therapy with stutterers (Doctoral dissertation, Teachers College, Columbia University, 1979). *Dissertation Abstracts International*, 1979, 39(11-B), 5569.

Meichenbaum, D., & Goodman, J. Training impulsive children to talk to themselves: A means of developing self-control. *Journal of Abnormal Psychology*, 1971, 77, 115-126.

Minskoff, E. H. Creating and evaluating remediation for the learning disabled. *Focus on Exceptional Children*, 1973, 5, 1-11.

Minuchin, S. Conflict-resolution family therapy. *American Orthopsychiatric Journal*, 1965, *28*, 278-286.

Mitchell, L. S. *Our children and our schools*. New York: Charles Scribner's Sons, 1950.

Moras, K., & Strupp, H. A. Pretherapy interpersonal relations, patients' alliance and outcome in brief therapy. *Archives of General Psychiatry*, 1982, *39*(4), 405-409.

National Institute of Neurological Diseases and Blindness. *Monograph #3*. U.S. Department of Health, Education and Welfare, 1966, p. 8.

Newton, J. R. The impact of relationship context and compatibility on communication effectiveness (Doctoral dissertation, Georgia State University College of Arts & Sciences, 1981). *Dissertation Abstracts International*, 1981, *41*(10-B), 3875.

Norman, W. B. Relationship factors in the counseling dyad (Journal article, Texas Technical University, 1977). *Dissertation Abstracts International*, 1977, *37*(10-B), 5368.

O'Leary, L. D. Behavior modification in the classroom: A rejoinder to Winett and Winkler. *Journal of Applied Behavior Analysis*, 1972, 5, 505-511.

O'Leary, K. D., & Drabman, R. M. Token reinforcement programs in the classroom. *Psychological Bulletin*, 1971, 75, 379-398.

Packer, J., & Bain, J. D. Cognitive style and teacher-student compatibility (Journal article, University of Queensland, Brisbane, Australia, 1978). *Journal of Educational Psychology*, 1978, *70*(5), 864-871.

Palkes, H., Stewart, M., & Freedman, J. Improvement of hyperactive boys as a function of verbal-training procedures. *Journal of Special Education*, 1972, *5*, 337-342.

Palkes, H., Stewart, M., & Kahana, B. Porteus maze performance of hyperactive boys after training self-directed verbal commands. *Child Development*, 1968, *39*, 817-826.

Pasamanick, B., & Knobloch, H. The epidemiology of reproductive casualty. In D. A. vanKrevelen (Ed.), *Child psychiatry*. Bern, Switzerland: Hans Huber Publishers, 1964, 108-115.

Paul, O. D. The relationship of student-teacher compatibility on student achievement in algebra (Journal article, Auburn University, 1973). *Dissertation Abstracts International*, 1973, *34*(3-A), 1180.

Pearson, G. H. S. Summary of learning difficulties. *Psychoanalytic Study of the Child* (Vol. 7). New York: International Universities Press, 1952.

Penman, R. *Communication processes and relationships*. London: Academic Press, 1980.

Peters, M. W. Client-counselor similarity and counseling outcome in a juvenile diversion program (Doctoral dissertation, Claremont University Center, 1980). *Dissertation Abstracts International*, 1980, *40*(9-B), 4499.

Piaget, J. *The language and thought of the child*. New York: Meridian Books, 1926 and 1955.

Piaget, J. *Judgment and reasoning of the child*. New York: Basic Books, 1928.

Piaget, J. *Child's conception of the world*. Patterson, NJ: Littlefield, Ames & Co., 1929.

Piaget, J. *The child's conception of physical causality*. New York: Harcourt Brace & Co., 1930.

Piaget, J. *The moral judgment of the child* (1st American Ed.). Glencoe, IL: Free Press, 1948.

Piaget, J. *Play, dreams and imitation in childhood*. New York: Norton, 1951.

Piaget, J. *The origins of intelligence in children* (2nd Ed.). New York: International Universities Press, 1952.

Piaget, J. *The construction of reality in the child*. New York: Basic Books, 1954.

Piaget, J. The stages of intellectual development of the child. *Bulletin of The Menninger School of Psychiatry*, March 6, 1961.

Piaget, J. The relation of affectivity to intelligence in the mental development of the child. *Bulletin of the Menninger Clinic*, 1962, *26*, 129-137.

Piaget, J. Appendix. In L.S. Vygotsky, *Thought and language*. Cambridge, MA: MIT Press and Wiley, 1962.

Piaget, J. *Psychology of intelligence*. Totowa, NJ: Littlefield, Adams, 1966.

Piaget, J. *The mechanics of perception*. New York: Basic Books, 1969.

Piaget, J., & Inhelder, B. *The child's conception of space*. London: Rutledge, Kegan, Paul, 1956.

Piaget, J., & Inhelder, B. *Memory and intelligence*. New York: Basic Books, 1968.

Piaget, J., & Inhelder, B. *The psychology of the child*. New York: Basic Books, 1969.

Posner, G. J. The extensiveness of curriculum structure: A conceptual scheme. *Review of Educational Research*, 1974, *44*, 401-407.

Pulakos, E. D., & Wexley, K. N. The relationship among perceptual similarity, sex, and performance ratings in manager subordinate dyads (Journal article, Michigan State University, 1983). *Academy of Management Journal*, 1983, *26*(1), 129-139.

Quay, H. C., Werry, J. S., McQueen, M., & Sprague, R. I. Remediation of the conduct problem child in the special class setting. *Exceptional Child*, 1966, *32*, 509-515.

Rapaport, D. The structure of psychoanalytic theory: A systematic attempt. *Psychological Issues*, 1960, Monograph 6.

Richardson, S. A. Psychosocial factors contributing to deprivation in child development. *Deprivation and Psychological Development. A Report of the Pan American Conference of the World Health Organization*, 1966, *134*, 55-65.

Rodriquez, R. *Hunger of memory*. New York: Bantam Books, 1982.

Rosenblum, L. A., & Youngstein, K. P. Developmental changes in compensatory dyadic response in mother and infant monkeys. In M. Lewis & L. A. Rosenblum (Eds.), *The effect of the infant on its caregiver*. New York: John Wiley, 1974.

Routh, D. K., & Mesibov, G. Psychological and environmental intervention toward social competence. In H. Rie and R. Rie (Eds.), *Handbook of minimal brain dysfunctions: A critical view*. New York: John Wiley, 1980.

Sameroff, A., & Chandler, M. An editorial in the continuum of caretaking causality. Division on Developmental Psychology. *American Psychological Association Newsletter*, Winter 1973, *3*.

Sapir, S. *A pilot approach to the education of first grade public school children with problems in bodily schema, perceptual, motor and/or language development*. Grant #6-8275, Department of Health, Education and Welfare, U.S. Office of Education, Division of Handicapped Children and Youth. Document #8895, Photoduplication Services, Library of Congress, Washington, D.C., 1961.

Sapir, S. Learning disability and deficit-centered classroom training. In J. Hellmuth (Ed.), *Cognitive studies 2: Deficits in cognition*. New York: Brunner/Mazel, 1971, 324-337.

Sapir, S. Educational intervention. In H. Rie and E. Rie (Eds.), *Handbook of minimal brain dysfunctions: A critical view*. New York: John Wiley, 1980.

Sapir, S., & Nitzburg, A. *Children with learning problems*. New York: Brunner/Mazel, 1973.

Sapir, S. G., & Wilson, B. A developmental scale to assist in the prevention of learning disability. *Educational and Psychological Measurement*, 1967, *23*, 1061-1068.

Sapir, S., & Wilson, B. *A professional's guide to working with the learning-disabled child*. New York: Brunner/Mazel, 1978.

Schultz, E. W. The influence of teacher behavior and dyad compatibility on clinical gains in arithmetic tutoring. *Journal of Research in Mathematics Education*, 1972, *3*(1), 33-41.

Schutz, W. C. *The firo scales*. Palo Alto, CA: Consulting Psychologists Press, 1967.

Semmel, M. I. *Application of systematic classroom observation to the study and modification of pupil-teacher interactions in special education*. Bloomington Center for Innovation in Teaching the Handicapped. Indiana University, 1974.

Shapiro, E., & Biber, B. The education of young children: A developmental approach. In S. Sapir & A. Nitzburg (Eds.), *Chilaren with learning problems*. New York: Brunner/Mazel, 1973, 682-709.

Shavelson, R. *Decision analysis of teaching*. Los Angeles, CA: University of California, 1975.

Silverman, W. A. Mismatched attitudes toward neonatal death. *Hastings Report.* New Rochelle, NY: Halsted Press, 1982.

Skinner, B. F. *The behavior of organisms: An experimental analysis.* New York: Appleton-Century-Crofts, 1938.

Skinner, B. F. *The technology of teaching.* New York: Appleton-Century-Crofts, 1968.

Spitz, R. Anaclitic depression. *Psychoanalytic Study of the Child, Vol. 2.* New York: International University Press, 1946.

Staats, A. W., Staats, C. K., Schultz, R. E., & Wolf, M. The conditioning of textual responses using extrinsic reinforcers. *Journal of The Experimental Analysis of Behavior,* 1962, *5,* 33-40.

Stern, A. Interpersonal compatibility and counseling supervision (Doctoral dissertation, University of Missouri, 1979). *Dissertation Abstracts International,* 1979, *39*(10-A), 6040.

Strauss, A. A., & Lehtinen, L. E. *Psychopathology and education in the brain-injured child.* New York: Grune & Stratton, 1947.

Thomas, A., Chess, S., & Birch, H. *Temperament and behavior disorders in children.* New York: New York University Press, 1968.

Thomas, D., Ribich, F., & Freie, J. The relationship between psychological identification with instructors and student ratings of college courses (Journal article, Wartburg College, 1982). *Instructional Science,* 1982, *11*(2), 139-154.

Tuddenham, R. D. Jean Piaget and the world of the child. In S. Sapir & A. Nitzburg (Eds.), *Children with learning problems.* Brunner/Mazel, 1973, 80-98.

Underwood, W. J., & Krafft, J. Interpersonal compatibility and managerial work effectiveness: A test of the fundamental interpersonal relations orientation theory (Journal article, RCA Corp., New York, NY, 1973). *Journal of Applied Psychology,* 1973, *58*(1), 89-94.

Vygotsky, L. S. The problem of the cultural development of the child. *Journal of Genetic Psychology,* 1929, *36,* 415-434.

Vygotsky, L. S. *Thought and language.* Cambridge, MA: MIT Press and Wiley, 1962.

Vygotsky, L. S. Mind in society. In M. Cole, V. John-Steiner, S. Scribner, & E. Souberman, (Eds.), *The development of higher psychological processes.* (Cambridge, MA: Harvard University Press, 1978.

Walter, W. G. Human frontal lobe functions in regulation of active state. In A. R. Luria & E. D. Homskaya (Eds.), *Frontal lobes and regulation of psychological processes.* Moscow: Moscow University Press, 1966.

Walzer, S., & Richmond, J. The epidemiology of learning disorders. In H. Grossman (Ed.), *Pediatric Disorders of North America,* *20*(3). Philadelphia, PA: W. B. Saunders, 1973.

Weil, A. M. P. Children with minimal brain dysfunction. *Psychosocial Process Issues in Child Mental Health* (Jewish Board of Guardians), 1970, *1*(2), 80-97.

Werner, H. *Comparative psychology of mental development.* Chicago: Fallett, 1948.

Werner, H. The concept of development from a comparative and organismic point of view. In D. B. Harris (Ed.), *The concept of development.* Minneapolis: University of Minnesota Press, 1957.

Werner, H., & Kaplan, B. *Symbol formation: An organismic-developmental approach to language and expression of thought.* New York: John Wiley, 1963.

Werry, J. S., & Wollersheim, J. P. Behavior therapy with children: A broad overview. *Journal of the American Academy of Child Psychiatry,* April 1967, 7, 2.

Wertheimer, M. Gestalt theory. *Social Research,* 1944, *2*(1), 78-99.

Wetzel, C. G., Schwartz, D., & Vasu, E. S. Roommate compatibility: Is there an ideal relationship (Journal article, University of Mississippi, 1979). *Journal of Applied Social Psychology,* 1979, *9*(5), 432-445.

White, R. W. Motivation reconsidered: The concept of competence. *Psychological Review,* 1959, *66*(5), 297-333.

White, R. T. Learning hierarchies. *Review of Educational Research,* 1973, *43*, 361-375.

Winett, R. A., & Winkler, R. C. Current behavior modification in the classroom: Be still, be quiet, be docile. *Journal of Applied Behavior Analysis,* 1972, *5*, 499-504.

Winnicott, D. W. Transitional objects and transitional phenomena. *International Journal of Psychiatry,* 1953, *34*.

Wolff, P. H. The developmental psychologies of J. Piaget and psychoanalysis. *Psychological Issues,* 1960, *2*(1).

Wolpe, J. *Psychotherapy by reciprocal inhibition.* Stanford, CA: Stanford University Press, 1958.

Yarrow, M. R., Waxler, C. Z., & Scott, P. M. Child effects on adult behavior. *Developmental Psychology,* 1971, *5*, 300-311.

Ysseldyke, J. E. Diagnostic-prescriptive teaching: The search for aptitude treatment interactions. In L. Mann and D. Sabatino (Eds.), *The first review of special education.* Philadelphia, PA: JSE Press, 1973.

Zentall, S. S. Optimal stimulation as theoretical basis of hyperactivity. *American Journal of Orthopsychiatry,* 1975, *45*, 549-563.

# Index